Social Studies
Actual Size

36 Complete Lesson Plans!

Sunflower
education

Exceptional Books for Teachers and Parents™

A Great Way to Teach Social Studies!

Kids love making and interacting with these creative full-scale chalk drawings—it's the next-best thing to being there! *Actual Size—Social Studies* makes it easy for you and your students to accurately draw the Seven Wonders of the Ancient World, a viking ship, and even an Iroquois longhouse. Draw the *Mayflower* and the Statue of Liberty's torch—in actual size! Detailed lesson plans and precise blueprints guide you in creating experiences your students will never forget.

36 Complete Lesson Plans • 36 Accurate Blueprints

Part of the Actual Size Series of books!

Visit SunflowerEducation.net

Please feel free to photocopy the activity sheets in this book within reason. Sunflower Education grants teachers permission to photocopy the activity sheets from this book for educational use. This permission is granted to individual teachers and not entire schools or school systems. Please send any permissions questions to permissions@SunflowerEducation.net.

Visit **SunflowerEducation.net** for more great books!

Editorial   Sunflower Education

Design   Cynthia Hannon Design

Illustrations: Miranda Mueller

Photography:
Cover image, ©Aliaksei Sabelnikau/Shutterstock Images LLC
Interior images, Wikimedia Commons

ISBN-13: 978-1-937166-06-9
ISBN-10: 1-937166-06-6
Copyright ©2013
Sunflower Education
Printed in the U.S.A.

Table of Contents

The Seven Wonders of the Ancient World

The Old World

Native America

U.S. History

Historic Transportation

Warfare

American Landmarks

To the Teacher

Turn the playground into a landscape for learning—and get ready to have some fun! *Actual Size—Social Studies* brings high-interest social studies topics to life.

How *Actual Size—Social Studies* is Organized

Actual Size—Social Studies includes 36 delightful activities. Each one focuses on an actual size (full scale) or small-scale drawing or diagram of a high-interest social studies topic.

Each activity consist of two pages:
- The *Activity Page* provides teaching material for how to create and use the drawing or diagram.
- The *Plan Page* provides the blueprint for the drawing or diagram itself.

Materials Needed

The materials needed for each activity are listed in the Prepare section of each Activity Page. For most activities, the key tools are:
- sidewalk chalk (and lots of it!)
- a meter or yardstick
- a measuring tape and/or a measuring wheel
- a carpenter's square
- chalk line reel

A few activities require a string and stakes (for drawing circles and ellipses). Other activities that involve drawing small-scale diagrams require small-scale human figures or objects. These are included on the Plan Pages. You should plan on copying those pages and cutting them out.

How to Use this Book

You may wish to integrate these activities into your curriculum or you may wish to use them as standalone fun. Teachers have used these activities as:
- lesson/topic openers
- main lesson topics
- extension activities
- enrichment activities
- independent class rewards

To the Teacher

A general lesson cycle for using the *Actual Size—Social Studies* includes the following steps, detailed on each of the Activity Pages:

Prepare

Each Activity Page begins with "Prepare." There are two parts to Prepare: *Allow time* is the approximate amount of time the activity will take. *Gather materials* lists the materials you will need for the activity.

Focus

Each Activity Page follows Prepare with "Focus." Focus includes bellringer and/or background information about the topic to help you get students excited about the lesson.

Present

Each Activity Page follows Focus with "Present." Present provides step-by-step instructions for creating the drawing or diagram and leading your students in interacting with it. Here is where the real learning—and the real fun!—takes place. Depending on your situation, you may wish to create the drawing or diagram yourself or, more likely, to divvy up tasks among your students working individually or in groups or as a class. *Actual Size—Social Studies* can be used with children of all different ages; simply adjust the amount of help you give them as they draw the diagrams accordingly.

Many of the diagrams were drawn very simply so that they would be easier for children to replicate. If you wish, you can show students relevant photographs and paintings of their subject (included on the Activity Pages) to provide them with more detail. Older or more advanced students can add greater details to their illustrations. You will notice that several of the projects are very large. Depending on the space and time you have available, you may want to draw some of these diagrams or drawings at half or quarter scale.

Notice any boldfaced vocabulary terms that you may integrate into the activity At the end of Present is a list of the vocabulary term(s) with concise definitions that you can share with your students.

KEY: Above all else, make sure that kids have the freedom to wander in and out of what they created, play (younger children enjoy make-believing), ask questions, and simply enjoy themselves. Essentially, you have just led them in creating a two-dimensional (and sometimes three-dimensional) specialized playscape. Let them have fun!

Conclude

Each Activity Page ends with "Conclude." Here you will find ways to wind the lesson down, questions for you and the students to discuss, or extension activities. They can help students concretize the ideas they encountered during the activity.

To the Teacher

Pedagogy

The activities in *Actual Size—Social Studies* fall under many pedagogical categories. These activities are kinesthetic, multisensory, interdisciplinary, concrete, accommodating, converging, diverging, assimilating "hands-on," project-based, grouped, and so on. Depending on your focus, and your pedagogical leanings, any of these aspects can be highlighted.

However you categorize the activities, though, the research is clear: the activities in *Actual Size—Social Studies* are pedagogically sound. According to the U.S. Department of Education, "the use of multiple representations—pictures, diagrams, charts and models—helps students visualize and understand difficult concepts." Further, "research has found that when teachers make connections between abstract and concrete representations, students are better able to apply what they have learned across a range of situations."

But, a simpler test is this: ask an adult to recall something from their own school days. Chances are, it will be a project or an activity. *Actual Size—Social Studies* is designed to help you create projects and lead activities that your students will find, literally, unforgettable!

We had one teacher share this about her experience: "My students got to see the fruits of their labor in just one class. It made them feel confident in themselves and in their imaginations."

Confident kids—is there anything better?

Care to share? We would love to see pictures of your students' creations. Please email them to info@SunflowerEducation.net.

You can also learn about *Actual Size—Science,* the companion book to *Actual Size—Social Studies.*

Visit SunflowerEducation.net

Grab some chalk and get ready for some fun!

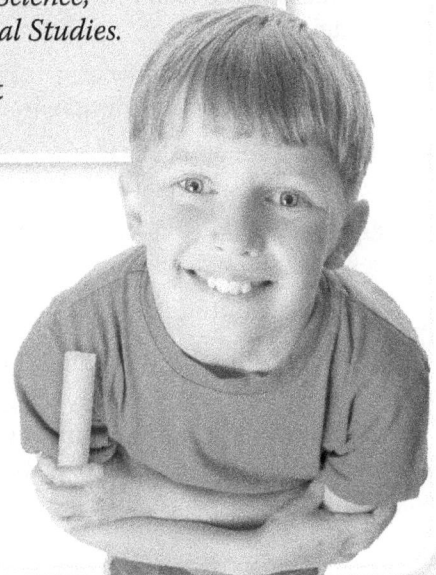

Vocabulary Terms

Every activity in *Actual Size—Social Studies* introduces students to one or more important vocabulary terms. Here they all are in one place.

amphibious: suited for both land and water

amphitheater: a large and round open-air theater

ancestor: someone from whom a person is descended

arithmetic: addition, subtraction, multiplication, and division

armored: covered with metal plates for protection

astronomical: having to do with the Sun, Moon, and stars

atlatl: a tool used to throw darts farther

authority: the power to lead people

awe: a feeling of respect, wonder, and sometimes fear towards something bigger than yourself

canvas: a type of strong cloth

chinking: a mixture of mud and straw used to fill gaps in a log cabin

colonize: when a group of people moves to a different land to create a new settlement

colossus: a statue of gigantic size

commemorate: to show respect for someone's memory

commercial: having to do with commerce or trade

cross section: the view that results when you cut through a three-dimensional object

curtain wall: a wall that surrounds a castle and usually links towers together

dignity: a quality that makes a person worthy of respect

domed: a vaulted roof

drainage: a way of removing, or taking away, extra water

duckboard: board made up of several wooden slats used to provide a dry path over muddy ground

dynamite: an explosive often used in mining and demolition

elementary: a school that teaches the first few grades

ellipse: an oval shape

empire: several different countries that are ruled by one government

engine: a machine that changes energy into motion

environment: the type of place in which one lives

executive branch: the branch of the government that carries out laws

explore: to look for something or somewhere new

fire-step: a place in a trench where a soldier can stand to look out at the field and fire his gun

fleet: a group of ships

foundation: the lowest level that holds up a building or structure

frontier: the edge of settled territory

gladiator: a man trained to fight other men or animals for entertainment

goods: items that have value

Greek mythology: the stories and legends Ancient Greeks had about their many gods and goddesses, heroes, and the nature of the world

henge: a prehistoric human structure made in the shape of a circle at least 65 feet in diameter

hide: skin

hull: the main body of a ship, including the bottom and sides that touch the water

immigrant: a person who moves from another country

independence: being free from outside control

inhospitable: not friendly or welcoming

Vocabulary Terms

invasion: when an army or group of people enters a country by force

Iroquois: A group of different Native American tribes who lived in the northeastern United States and parts of Canada

lighthouse: a tower or building that shines light from a system of lamps and lenses (or in older times, from a fire) to guide ships at sea

locomotive: a vehicle able to move itself and other parts of a train; engine

loft: a high platform used for storage or for extra living space

mausoleum: a large, often richly decorated tomb or building housing a tomb or several tombs

medieval: from the Middle Ages, c. 500-1500 CE

melting pot: a place where many different kinds of people live together and share a culture

mission: headquarters for people who are trying to spread the Christian religion

Mississippi River: a very large American river

moat: a deep, wide ditch filled with water that surrounds and protects a castle

monument: a structure built to commemorate a famous person or event

nomads: a group of people who don't have a fixed home

pedestal: a supporting structure or piece

Pilgrims: a group of people who left Europe on the *Mayflower* in search of religious freedom

pioneer: one of the first people to settle in a new place

podium: a wall forming a base of a structure

prairie: an area of land covered in grass

President of the United States: the head of the executive branch of the government of the United States

propeller: a mechanical device that propels an airplane by spinning blades through the air

religious freedom: the freedom for people or communities to practice the religion they choose

Scandinavia: an area of northern Europe that includes Norway, Sweden, Denmark, Finland, and Iceland

bow: the front end of a ship

schooner: a type of sailboat

sculpture: a three-dimensional work of art

scurvy: a disease caused by not getting enough vitamin C, often suffered by early sailors

sign language: a way of communicating to someone by using movements of the hands and arms

Sioux: A Native American tribe that originally lived in the Western and Midwestern United States

smokestack: a chimney that removes smoke from a locomotive or ship

stalemate: a situation where there is no clear winner or loser

stance: the way someone stands

symbol: something that represents or stands for something else

technology: using science for practical purposes

parallel: lines that are side by side and have the same distance between every part of themselves

ton: 2,000 pounds

transportation: a way of getting from one place to another

vault: an arched structure forming a ceiling or roof

irrigation: a system to supply water to a dry area by means of ditches or pipes; the watering of plants

vegetation: plants

The Seven Wonders of the Ancient World

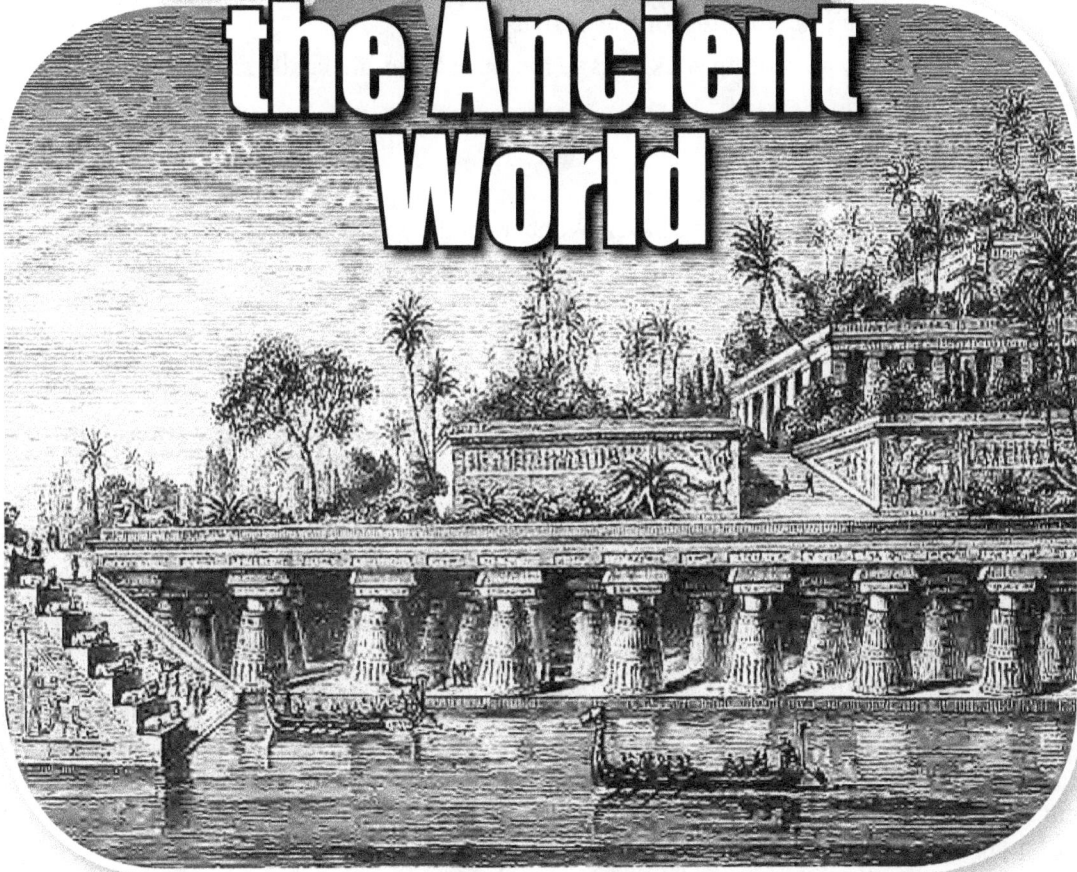

The Lighthouse of Alexandria

Students create a scale model of the Lighthouse of Alexandria and learn how far its light could shine.

Prepare

- *Allow time:* approximately 45 minutes for this activity
- *Gather materials:* Plan 1, measuring stick or tape measure, sidewalk chalk, scale figure

Focus

The Lighthouse of Alexandria is one of the Seven Wonders of the Ancient World. The Seven Wonders of the Ancient World were identified by Greek travelers during the 4th century BCE. The Lighthouse of Alexandria was built on the island of Pharos in Alexandria, Egypt between 285 and 247 BCE. It was the first *lighthouse* in the world, and it stood for 1,500 years. Historians think that the lighthouse was damaged by massive earthquakes throughout the centuries and collapsed in about 1326 CE. It was the last of the ancient wonders to disappear.

Ask students what they know about lighthouses. Point out that lighthouses are not as common today as they used to be because of newer navigation systems, such as radar and the Global Positioning System (GPS).

Present

❶ Consult Plan 1. On the playground (or appropriate indoor floor), draw a 6-foot line. Have students individually or in groups draw a picture of the lighthouse using the line as a guideline. Ensure that their drawing tapers towards the top. Then have students lay the scale figure next to their drawing to see how big an adult would be next to the lighthouse.

❷ Explain to students that the Lighthouse of Alexandria used a giant mirror to reflect the sunlight during the day and fire at night to guide ships safely into the harbor. Ask them how far they think the light from their model of the Lighthouse of Alexandria would shine.

❸ Tell students that some ancient sources claim that the light from the Lighthouse of Alexandria could be seen 35 miles away. Tell students that the distance at the scale of their drawing would be more than half a mile!

—————————————— *Vocabulary* ——————————————

lighthouse: a tower or building that shines light from a system of lamps and lenses (or in older times, from a fire) to guide ships at sea

Conclude

Discuss the students' estimates on how far the light could be seen. Discuss how people who lived long ago were as intelligent as people are today and achieved great feats of engineering.

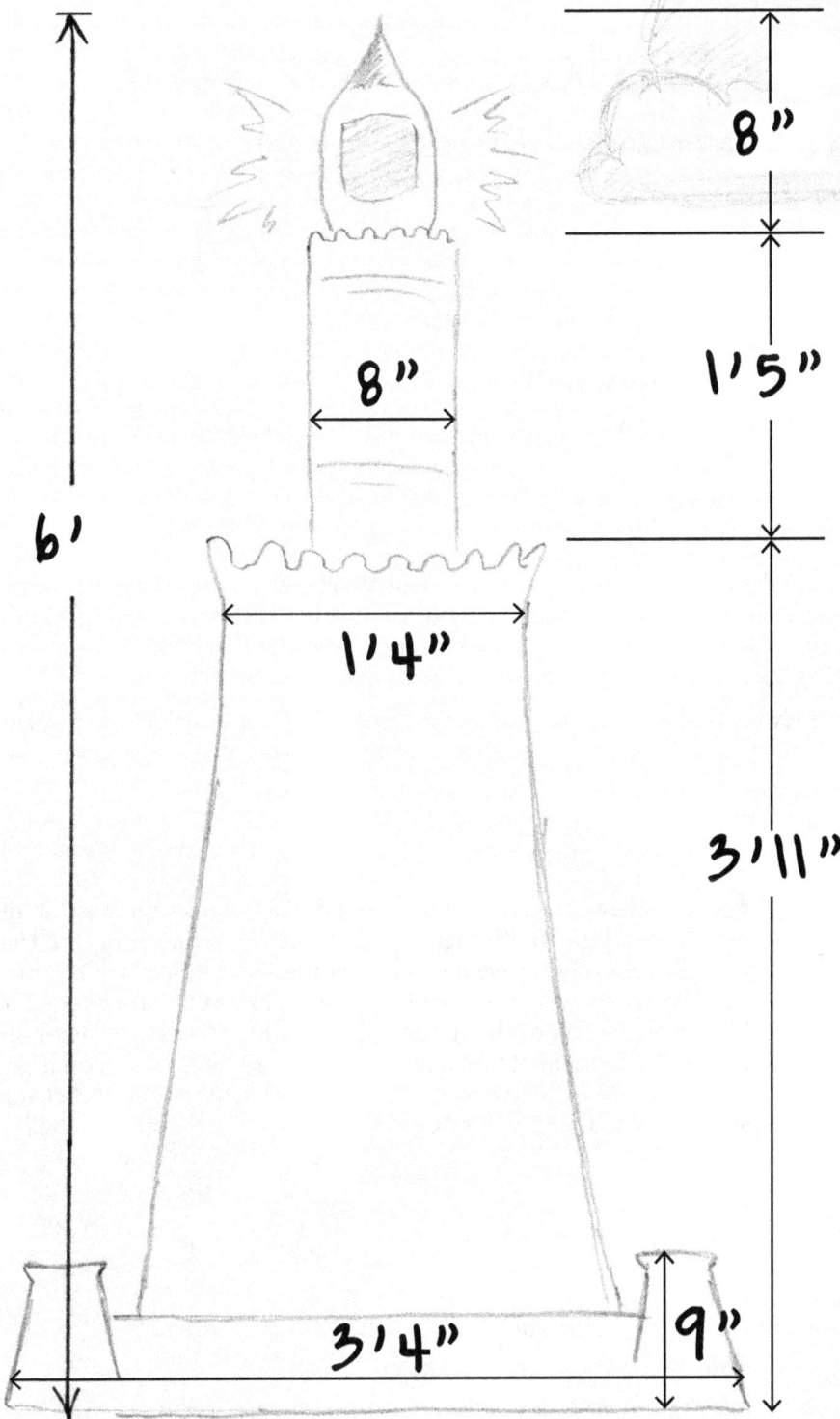

8"

1'5"

8"

6'

1'4"

3'11"

1" figure
**Actual height
6 feet**

9"

3'4"

Actual Size Social Studies

Lighthouse of Alexandria

Actual Size: 400' tall | PLAN 1

SUNFLOWEREDUCATION.NET

The Colossus of Rhodes

Students recreate the Colossus of Rhodes in order to appreciate how big the statue was.

Prepare

- *Allow time:* approximately 2 hours for this activity
- *Gather materials:* Plan 2, measuring tape or measuring wheel, sidewalk chalk, chalk line

Focus

The *Colossus* of Rhodes is one of the Seven Wonders of the Ancient World. The Seven Wonders of the Ancient World were identified by Greek travelers during the 4th century BCE. The Colossus of Rhodes was located on the Greek island of Rhodes and was built sometime between 304 and 292 BCE. The statue stood for about 56 years until it fell and broke apart due to an earthquake.

Ask students to discuss what they think statues are made from. Discuss different possible materials—such as marble, metal, stone, and bronze. Explain that this particular statue was made from bronze.

Present

❶ Consult Plan 2. On the playground (or appropriate indoor floor), have students work in pairs to measure out and draw one 110-foot line using the measuring wheel and chalk line. Have students draw a man standing up who is as tall as the line they drew. As the *stance* of the Colossus is unknown, encourage student creativity.

❷ Next, have one student lie next to the statue (with their feet aligned). Then have his/her partner draw an outline of his/her body next to the statue. Encourage students to imagine what it would be like to look up at a statue of a man that tall.

❸ Explain to students that this statue stood on a *pedestal*. Have students estimate how big the pedestal would have needed to be. Tell students that historians think the statue stood on a huge white marble pedestal that was perhaps 50 feet tall. Also tell them that the statue was so big that grown-ups could barely wrap their arms around the statue's thumb!

———————————— Vocabulary ————————————

colossus: a statue of gigantic size
stance: the way someone stands
pedestal: a supporting structure or piece

Conclude

Lead a discussion about why people create large works of art like statues and murals.

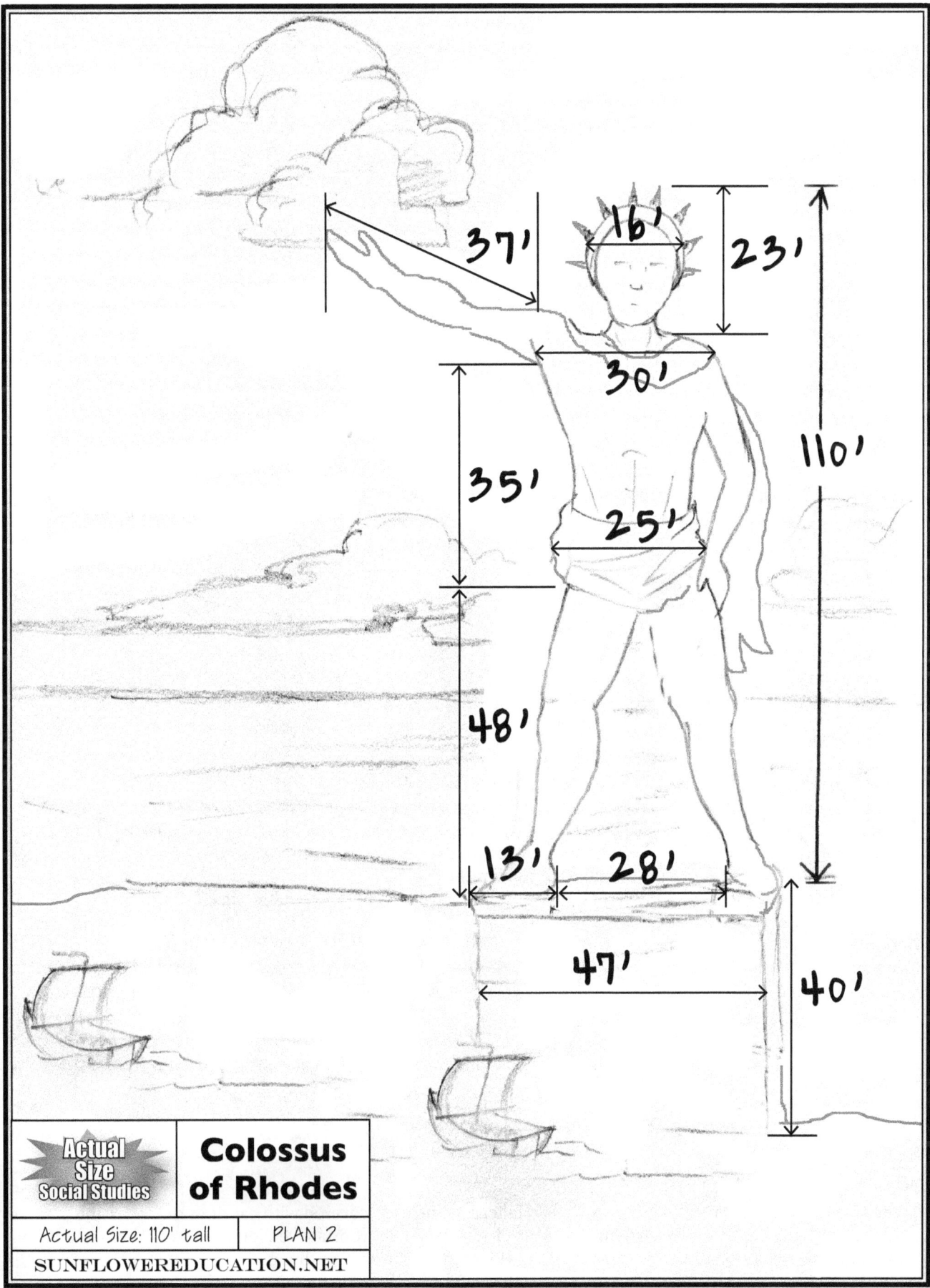

37'

16'

23'

30'

110'

35'

25'

48'

13'

28'

47'

40'

Actual Size Social Studies

Colossus of Rhodes

Actual Size: 110' tall | PLAN 2

SUNFLOWEREDUCATION.NET

The Mausoleum at Halicarnassus

Students recreate the Mausoleum at Halicarnassus in order to see the size of this ancient wonder.

Prepare

- *Allow time:* approximately 1 hour for this activity
- *Gather materials:* Plan 3, measuring tape or measuring wheel, sidewalk chalk, chalk line, carpenter's square

Focus

The *Mausoleum* is one of the Seven Wonders of the Ancient World. The Seven Wonders of the Ancient World were identified by Greek travelers during the 4th century BCE. The Mausoleum at Halicarnassus was located in Halicarnassus, which is now Bodrum, Turkey. The Mausoleum was built around 353 BCE. It was built as a tomb for Mausolus, who ruled Halicarnassus from 377 to 353 BCE. This was the first Mausoleum, and the word mausoleum comes from Mausolus' name.

Discuss how many years are in a century. Discuss how old modern buildings are (e.g., the U.S. Capitol building was built in 1793; the Empire State Building was built in 1931.) Explain to students that the Mausoleum at Halicarnassus stood for more than *16 centuries* before it was shattered by several earthquakes.

Present

❶ Consult Plan 3. On the playground (or appropriate indoor floor), draw a 93-foot line using the measuring wheel and chalk line; draw an 80-foot line at a right angle at one end of the first line using the carpenter's square. Then complete the rectangle. Draw a 47-foot line straight up from the middle of one of the 80-foot sides. Connect the top of this line to the two closest corners of the rectangle. This represents the Mausoleum as seen from the side.

❷ Explain to students that the Mausoleum at Halicarnassus had four parts. The lowest part of the rectangle was a *podium* that supported the rest of the Mausoleum. Above the podium there was a row of columns all the way around the Mausoleum. Above the columns, the Mausoleum had a pyramidal roof which was a statue of a chariot. Around this whole structure ran a wall that formed a perimeter.

——————————— Vocabulary ———————————

mausoleum: a large, often richly decorated tomb or building housing a tomb or several tombs
podium: a wall forming a base of a structure

Conclude

The sides of the podium of the Mausoleum at Halicarnassus were covered with carvings of battles and important events from Greek mythology. Tell students an age-appropriate version of a Greek myth and have them draw images from this story on the wall of the Mausoleum they outlined.

Mausoleum at Halicarnassus

Actual Size: 140' tall	PLAN 3

SUNFLOWEREDUCATION.NET

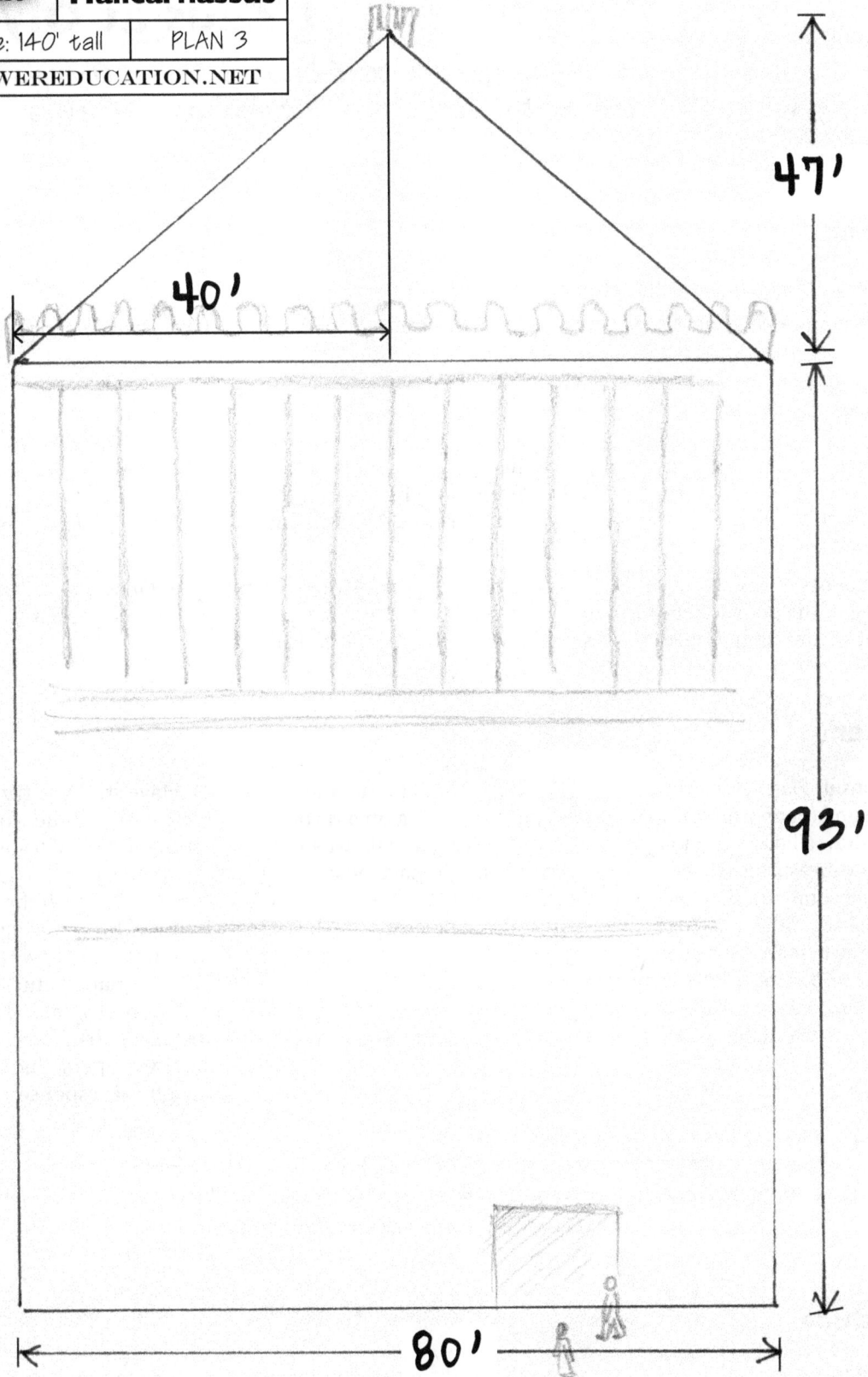

40'

47'

93'

80'

The Statue of Zeus at Olympia

Students recreate the Statue of Zeus at Olympia in order to visualize how imposing the statue was.

Prepare

- *Allow time:* approximately 1½ hours for this activity
- *Gather materials:* Plan 4, measuring tape or measuring wheel, sidewalk chalk, chalk line, carpenter's square

Focus

The Statue of Zeus at Olympia is one of the Seven Wonders of the Ancient World. The Seven Wonders of the Ancient World were identified by Greek travelers during the 4th century BCE. The Statue of Zeus was located in Olympia, Greece and was built around 432 BCE by the Greek sculptor Phidias. It was destroyed sometime around 425 CE.

Ask students to discuss what they know about Zeus and Mount Olympus. In *Greek mythology,* Zeus was the king of the gods, ruler of Mount Olympus, and the god of the sky and thunder. Mount Olympus is the highest mountain in Greece. It was believed that the Greek gods lived there.

Present

❶ Consult Plan 4. On the playground (or appropriate indoor floor), draw a line 39 feet long using the measuring wheel and chalk line; draw another line 22 feet long at a right angle to the end of the first line using the carpenter's square. Then complete the rectangle. Using Plan 4 as a guide, have students draw an outline of the Statue of Zeus at Olympia inside the rectangle.

❷ This statue of Zeus was sculpted as sitting on a throne. Discuss with students why the sculptor might have posed Zeus in this way. What kinds of things does sitting in a throne tell you?

❸ Have students try to estimate how tall the statue would be if Zeus stood up. An ancient Greek remarked that it looked like Zeus would crash through the ceiling of his temple if he were to stand up! Discuss with students how this giant statue must have looked to people in the ancient world, who had never seen things like skyscrapers. Encourage thoughtful responses.

————————————— *Vocabulary* —————————————

Greek mythology: the stories and legends Ancient Greeks had about their many gods and goddesses, heroes, and the nature of the world

Conclude

Explain to students that the statue was destroyed a long time ago and that its precise measurements have been lost. Talk with students about how such basic information about a famous statue could disappear.

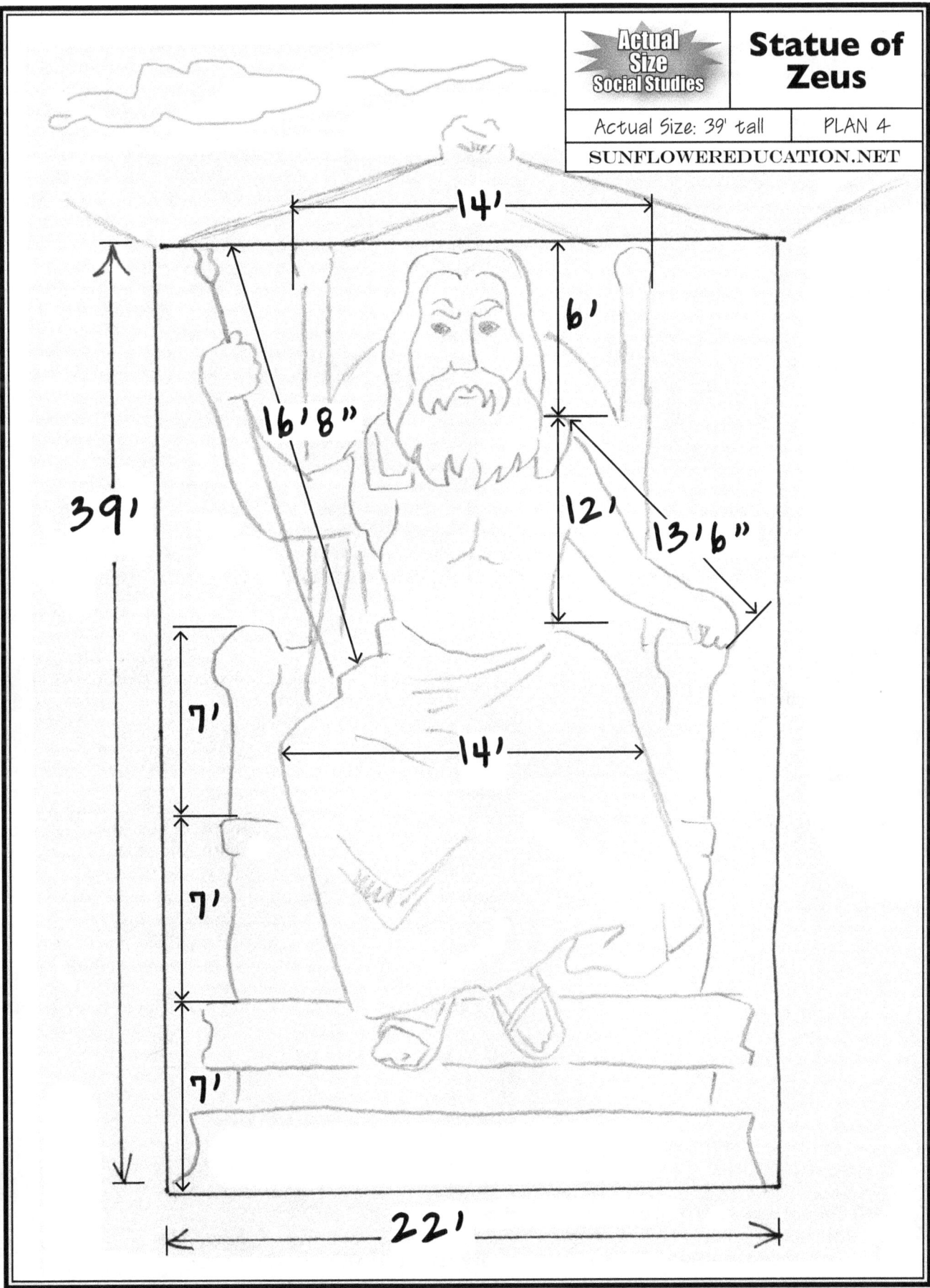

14'

6'

16'8"

12'

13'6"

39'

7'

14'

7'

7'

22'

Activity 5

The Temple of Artemis at Ephesus

Students create a scale model of the Temple of Artemis in order to appreciate its actual size.

Prepare

- *Allow time:* approximately 45 minutes for this activity
- *Gather materials:* Plan 5, measuring tape or measuring wheel, sidewalk chalk, chalk line, carpenter's square, scale figure

Focus

The Temple of Artemis is one of the Seven Wonders of the Ancient World. The Seven Wonders of the Ancient World were identified by Greek travelers during the 4th century BCE. The Temple of Artemis was located near the ancient city of Ephesus, south of the modern port city of Izmir, Turkey. It was built around 650 BCE. The temple was a tribute to Artemis, the Greek goddess of the hunt. The temple was destroyed by fire around 356 BCE.

Ask students to discuss how long it takes to build structures today. Explain that a typical house can be built in anywhere from two months to a year. Explain that the Dallas Cowboy football stadium, which is the largest *domed* stadium in the world, took more than three years to build. Explain to students that historians believe it took more than 120 years to complete the Temple of Artemis.

Present

❶ Consult Plan 5. On the playground (or appropriate indoor floor), draw an 11-foot line using the measuring wheel and chalk line; draw another, 5-foot line at a right angle to the end of the first line using the carpenter's square. Then complete the rectangle. Have a student place a copy of the scale figure upright just outside the rectangle. This is how big an average adult would be next to the Temple of Artemis.

❷ Explain to students that the temple had many columns that went all the way around the perimeter of the structure. Have the students estimate how many columns it would take to go around the entire temple. A total of 127 columns enclosed the center of the temple. Each was 60 feet tall—the height of ten of the scale figures!

——————————— *Vocabulary* ———————————
domed: a vaulted roof

Conclude

The Temple of Artemis was huge. Three football fields could fit inside of it! What is even more amazing is that, other than the roof, the entire temple was made of marble—a very heavy, beautiful stone. Point out that the ancient Greeks did not have any of the heavy machinery we use today.

Fold

11'

5'

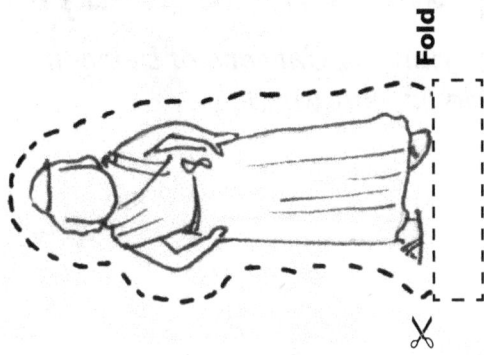

Activity 6
The Hanging Gardens of Babylon

Students recreate the Hanging Gardens of Babylon in order to visualize this ancient wonder.

Prepare

- *Allow time:* approximately 1 hour for this activity
- *Gather materials:* Plan 6, measuring tape or measuring wheel, sidewalk chalk, chalk line, carpenter's square

Focus

The Hanging Gardens of Babylon are one of the Seven Wonders of the Ancient World. The Seven Wonders of the Ancient World were identified by Greek travelers during the 4th century BCE. The Hanging Gardens were located in the east bank of the Euphrates River, about 50 miles South of today's Baghdad, Iraq. They were built around 600 BCE by the ruling king, Nebuchadnezzar. They were destroyed by earthquakes around the second century BCE.

Ask students to discuss what modern-day gardens look like. Explain that the Hanging Gardens were described as being built on a *vault*. The gardens were said to resemble a theater.

Present

❶ Consult Plan 6. On the playground (or appropriate indoor floor), draw one 100-foot baseline using the measuring wheel and chalk line. Draw an 80-foot straight line that is perpendicular to the middle of the first line using the carpenter's square, measuring wheel, and chalk line. Connect the top of this line with the two ends of the base to form an isosceles triangle. This will create a ¼-scale model of the Hanging Gardens.

❷ Have students draw representations of vaulted areas within the triangle (using Plan 6 as a guide). Explain that the actual dimensions of the vaulted areas of the Hanging Gardens are unknown. Have students suggest what they think the vaulted areas might have looked like– encourage creativity.

❸ Ask students what they know about taking care of a garden. Discuss the importance of watering a garden. Now, ask students how they would water their vaulted gardens. Have students brainstorm different ideas for *irrigation*.

——————— Vocabulary ———————
vault: an arched structure forming a ceiling or roof
irrigation: a system to supply water to a dry area by means of ditches or pipes; the watering of plants

Conclude

Explain to students that the ancient Babylonians probably used a chain pump to irrigate the Hanging Gardens. A chain pump carried water from a pool on the ground to a pool above the gardens in buckets attached to a large wheel. This wheel was turned by hand via another wheel.

Actual
Size
Social Studies

Hanging Gardens

Actual Size: ~320' tall | PLAN 6

SUNFLOWEREDUCATION.NET

80'

100'
Base

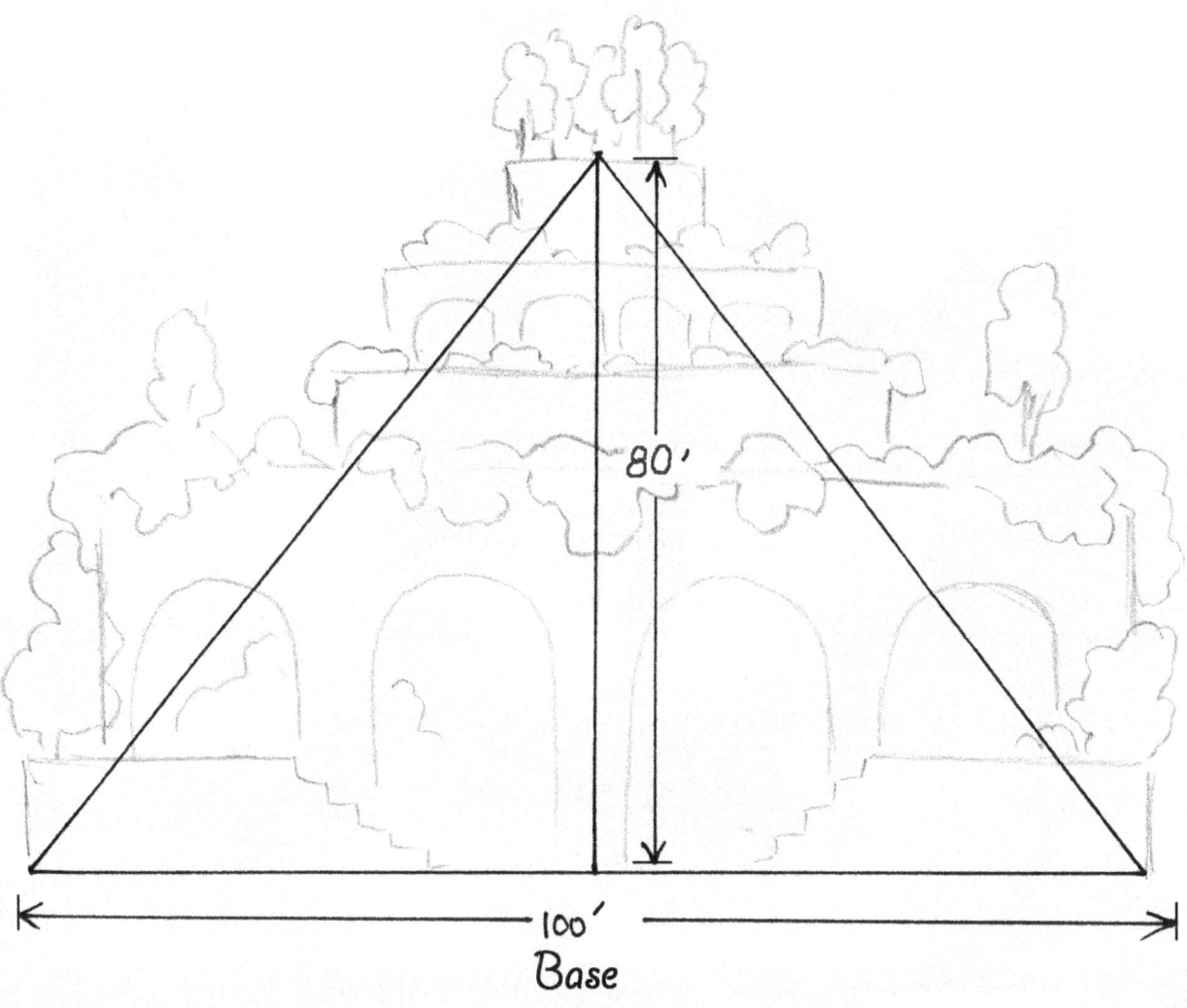

Activity 7
The Great Pyramid of Giza

Students create a scale drawing of the Great Pyramid of Giza in order to appreciate how big this wonder is.

Prepare

- *Allow time:* approximately 45 minutes for this activity
- *Gather materials:* Plan 7, measuring tape or measuring wheel, sidewalk chalk or chalk line, scale figure

Focus

The Pyramid of Giza is one of the Seven Wonders of the Ancient World. The Seven Wonders of the Ancient World were identified by Greek travelers during the 4th century BCE. The Pyramid of Giza is located in Cairo, Egypt and was built around 2560 BCE. It is the oldest of the Seven Wonders—the only Ancient Wonder that still stands today. The Pyramid of Giza held the record for tallest human-made structure for more than 3,800 years.

Ask students to discuss what they know about pyramids—what makes a pyramid a pyramid (the shape; the outer surfaces are triangular and meet at a point), what they were used for (usually they were used for tombs), where were they built (Egypt, China, North America, India), etc.

Present

❶ Consult Plan 7. On the playground (or appropriate indoor floor), draw a 22-foot baseline using the measuring tape or wheel and chalk line. Draw a 14-foot line perpendicular to the middle of the first line. Connect the top of this line with the two ends of the first line to create an isosceles triangle. Place the scale figure in a prone position at the base. That is how big a full-grown person is compared to the Great Pyramid of Giza. The real pyramid once stood about 480 feet tall, and each side of the base is about 756 feet long.

❷ Explain that each stone block of the pyramid weighs approximately two *tons,* and the Pyramid of Giza was constructed of nearly 2.5 million blocks. The blocks were carved from limestone.

❸ Have students discuss their ideas on how the pyramid was built. Tell students that historians think it most likely took more than 200,000 men close to 20 years to build the pyramid.

—————————— Vocabulary ——————————
ton: 2,000 pounds

Conclude

Locate Egypt on a map. Tell students that people travel from all over the world to see the pyramids of Egypt. Where do the students dream of travelling some day?

14´

22´

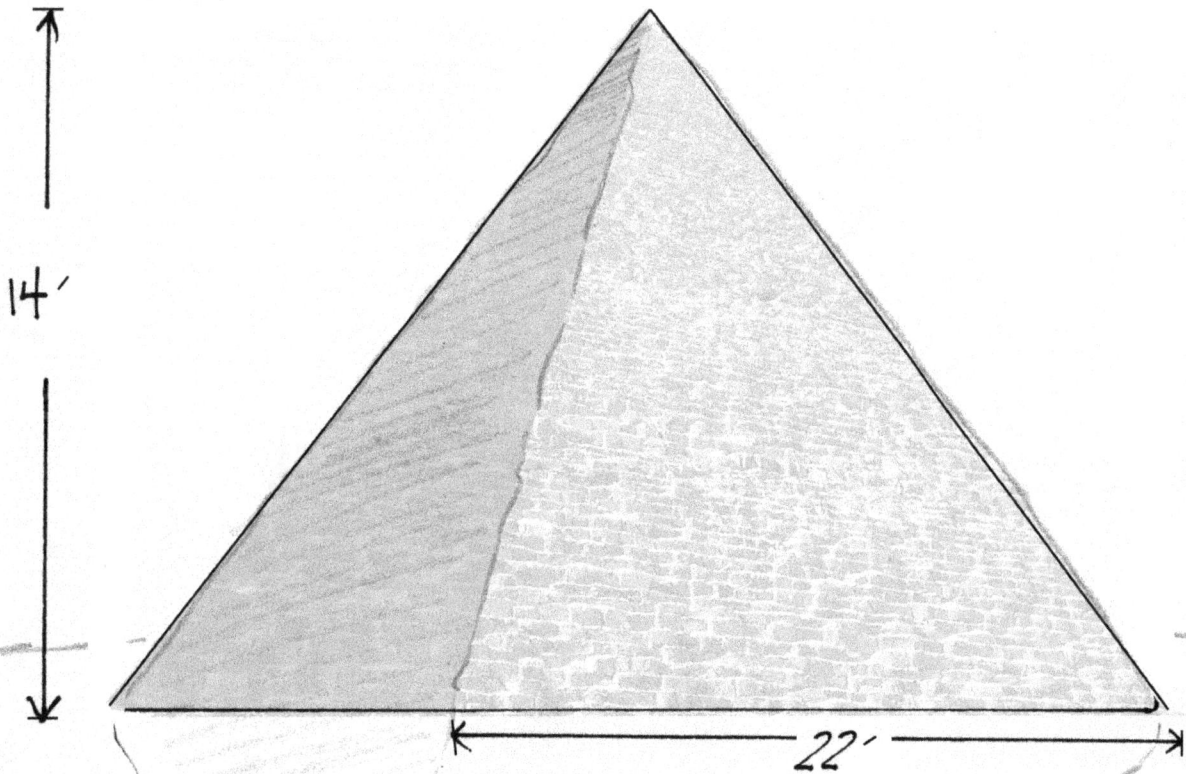

2" figure

The Old World

Stonehenge

Students outline the inner portion of Stonehenge in order to understand the size of this famous structure.

Prepare

- *Allow time:* approximately 1 hour for this activity
- *Gather materials:* Plan 8, measuring tape or measuring wheel, sidewalk chalk, carpenter's square, stake, string

Focus

Discuss calendars with students—what they are, what they're based on (the movement of Earth, Sun, and Moon), and how we use them. Explain that some ancient peoples also kept calendars by tracking the movement of the Sun, Moon, and stars. Stonehenge is one of the earliest examples of an *astronomical* calendar. It is also the most famous *henge* in the world.

Present

❶ Consult Plan 8. Cut a 54-foot-long piece of string. On the playground (or appropriate indoor floor), have a student hold one end of the string. Take the other end and pull it taught. Draw a circle as you walk around the student. This represents the ring of stones. From the center, measure 25 feet out. Draw a 50-foot line perpendicular to and centered on the end of this line. Draw 50-foot lines perpendicular to both ends of this line in the opposite direction of the 25-foot measurement. This will form a horseshoe shape to represent the innermost stones.

❷ Invite students into the drawing. There, discuss how and why a calendar would help ancient people. Point out that it is very helpful for farmers to know when the seasons change. With an astronomical calendar, you can figure out when the seasons are likely to change, so that you plant in the spring and harvest in the fall.

❸ People from all over the world have visited Stonehenge for a very long time. Explain to your class that what you drew was only the middle of Stonehenge. All of Stonehenge together is almost 2 miles across!

—————————— Vocabulary ——————————

astronomical: having to do with the Sun, Moon, and stars
henge: a prehistoric human structure made in the shape of a circle at least 65 feet in diameter

Conclude

One of the most interesting facts about Stonehenge is that the giant stones used to build it came from hundreds of miles away. Scientists have debated for a long time how exactly these stones were moved so far. Encourage children to brainstorm possible ways to move huge stones hundreds of miles with no heavy machinery, wheels, or horses. Explain to students that the most widely accepted theory is that the stones were rolled on top of tree trunks across all of those miles.

50´

50´

25´

50´

X

108´

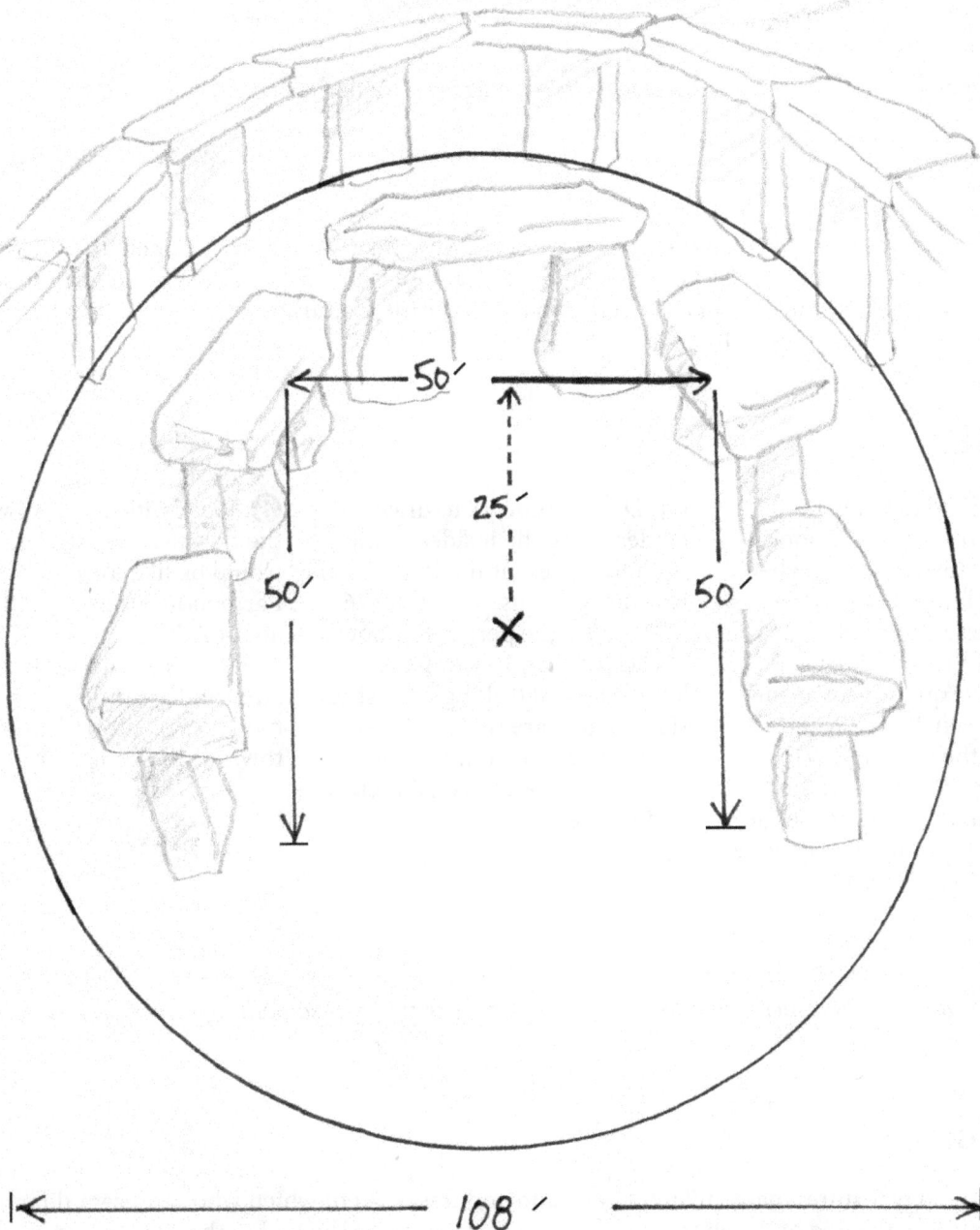

Activity 9
The Parthenon

Students outline the Parthenon in order to learn about Ancient Greek architecture and mythology.

Prepare

- *Allow time:* approximately 1 hour for this activity
- *Gather materials:* Plan 9, measuring tape or measuring wheel, sidewalk chalk, chalk line, carpenter's square

Focus

The ancient Greeks believed that their gods were very powerful. It is no wonder, then, that the Parthenon is so big! This temple is in Athens, Greece, and it was built for Athena, the Greek goddess of wisdom and justice. Though the Parthenon has been damaged over the centuries, much of the structure is still standing.

Present

❶ Consult Plan 9. On the playground, draw a 237-foot line using the measuring wheel and chalk line. Draw another, 110-foot line at a right angle to the end of the first line using the carpenter's square, measuring wheel, and chalk line. Then complete the rectangle. This represents an outline of the Parthenon. (Create a rectangle 113½ feet long and 55 feet wide for a half-size version.)

❷ Direct students to draw circles along the insides of the lines to represent the Parthenon's famous columns. There are 46 of them on the perimeter: one at each corner, 15 along each long side, and 6 along each short side. (There are several dozen more interior columns.) Circles should be about 6 feet, 2 inches in diameter.

❸ Walk with students within the outline. Ask students what it would be like to actually visit the Parthenon. How would they feel about Athena in a grand temple like that? Explain to students that large and beautiful temples were meant to create a feeling of *awe* towards the gods.

—————————————— *Vocabulary* ——————————————

awe: a feeling of respect, wonder, and sometimes fear towards something bigger than yourself

Conclude

Greek mythology features many different gods and goddesses, all of which who represent different things. Zeus was the god of the sky and of thunder, Poseidon was the god of the sea, and Aphrodite was the goddess of love. Explain to students that the Greeks told myths, or stories, about their gods and goddesses. In these stories, the gods were often like people, but they were much more powerful.

⭐ **Actual Size Social Studies**	**Parthenon**	
	Actual Size: 237' x 110'	PLAN 9
	SUNFLOWEREDUCATION.NET	

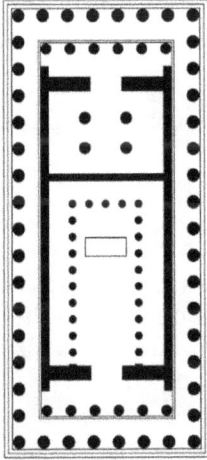

Top view showing interior walls and columns

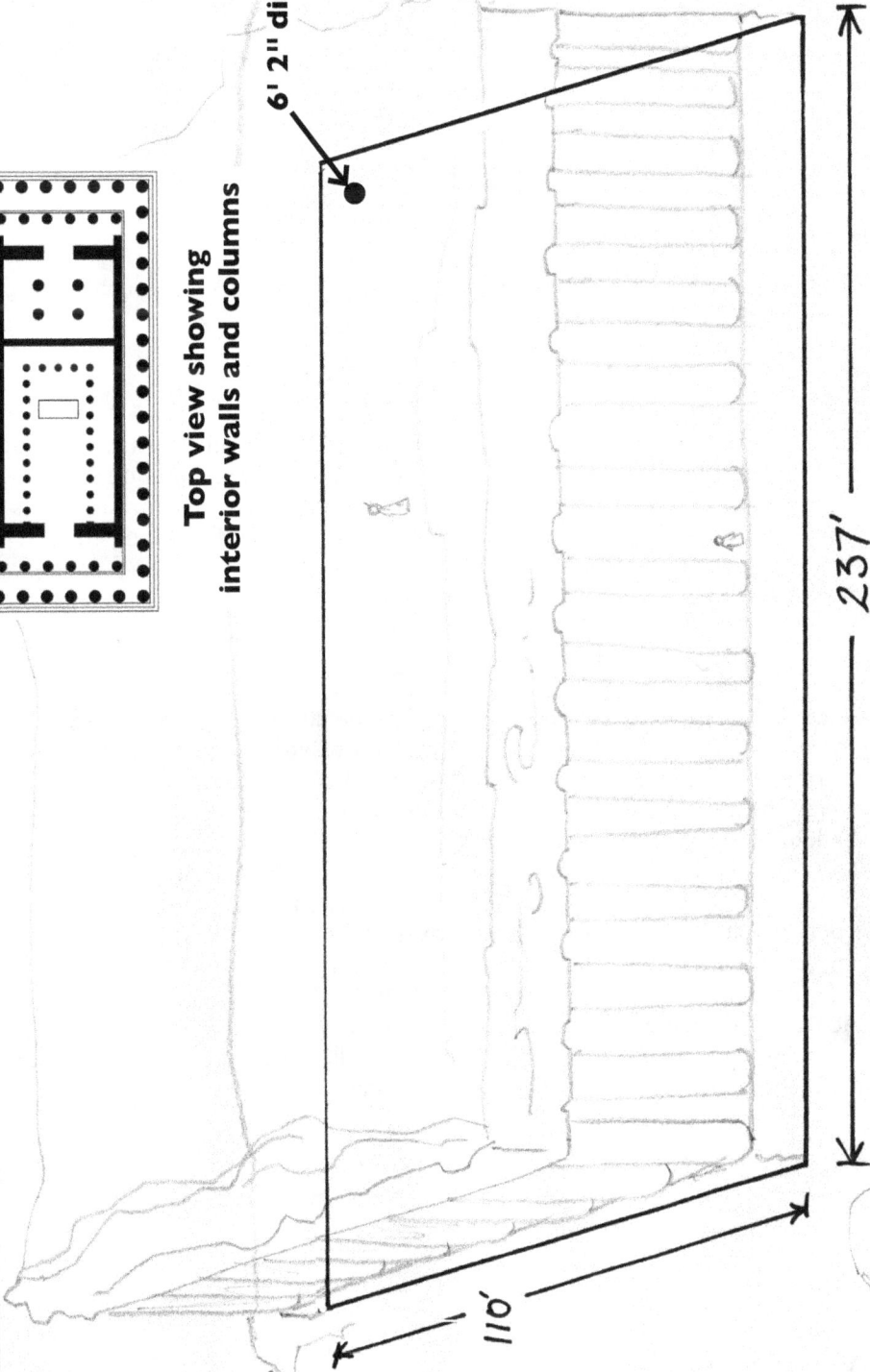

6' 2" diameter

237'

110'

Roman Roads

Students create a cross section of a Roman road in order to appreciate the importance of roads in Ancient Rome.

Prepare

- *Allow time:* approximately 1½ hours for this activity
- *Gather materials:* Plan 10, measuring tape, measuring wheel, sidewalk chalk, chalk line, carpenter's square

Focus

Have you ever heard the saying, "All roads lead to Rome"? At one time, it really was true. The Roman Empire was one of the most impressive empires in history, covering 25 million square miles around the Mediterranean Sea. The Romans needed a way to transport armies, settlers, and goods throughout their *empire*, and they built a system of roads that totaled about 50,000 miles—long enough to circle the Earth twice!

Present

❶ Consult Plan 10. On the playground (or appropriate indoor floor), draw a line that is 40 feet long using the measuring wheel and chalk line. Draw another 20-foot line at a right angle to one end of the first line using the carpenter's square, measuring wheel, and chalk line. This represents the surface of the road, which could be made up of gravel or stones. Draw two 10-inch lines, perpendicular downward from the 20-foot line. Each of these represents a layer of sand or gravel. Draw a third 10-inch line, which represents a *foundation* layer made up of large stones. Finally, draw a 20-inch line. This area formed represents a layer of dirt that has been packed down. Using Plan 10 as a guide, fill in the different layers. You might consider using different colors of chalk to represent different materials.

❷ Ask students why they think Romans would build roads in this way. Explain to them that the different layers made the roads strong enough to carry armies and travelers. They also provided *drainage* (note the ditches along the road), which is key to their longevity.

———————— Vocabulary ————————

empire: several different countries that are ruled by one government
foundation: the lowest level that holds up a building or structure
drainage: a way of removing, or taking away, extra water

Conclude

These roads were so well built that some of them are still in use today! Have students imagine walking on one of these roads. What would it be like to walk on a road that Roman soldiers had marched over thousands of years ago? Encourage thoughtful and creative responses.

40'

20'

10" **stone surface**

10" **sand or gravel**

10" **foundation stones**

20" **packed dirt**

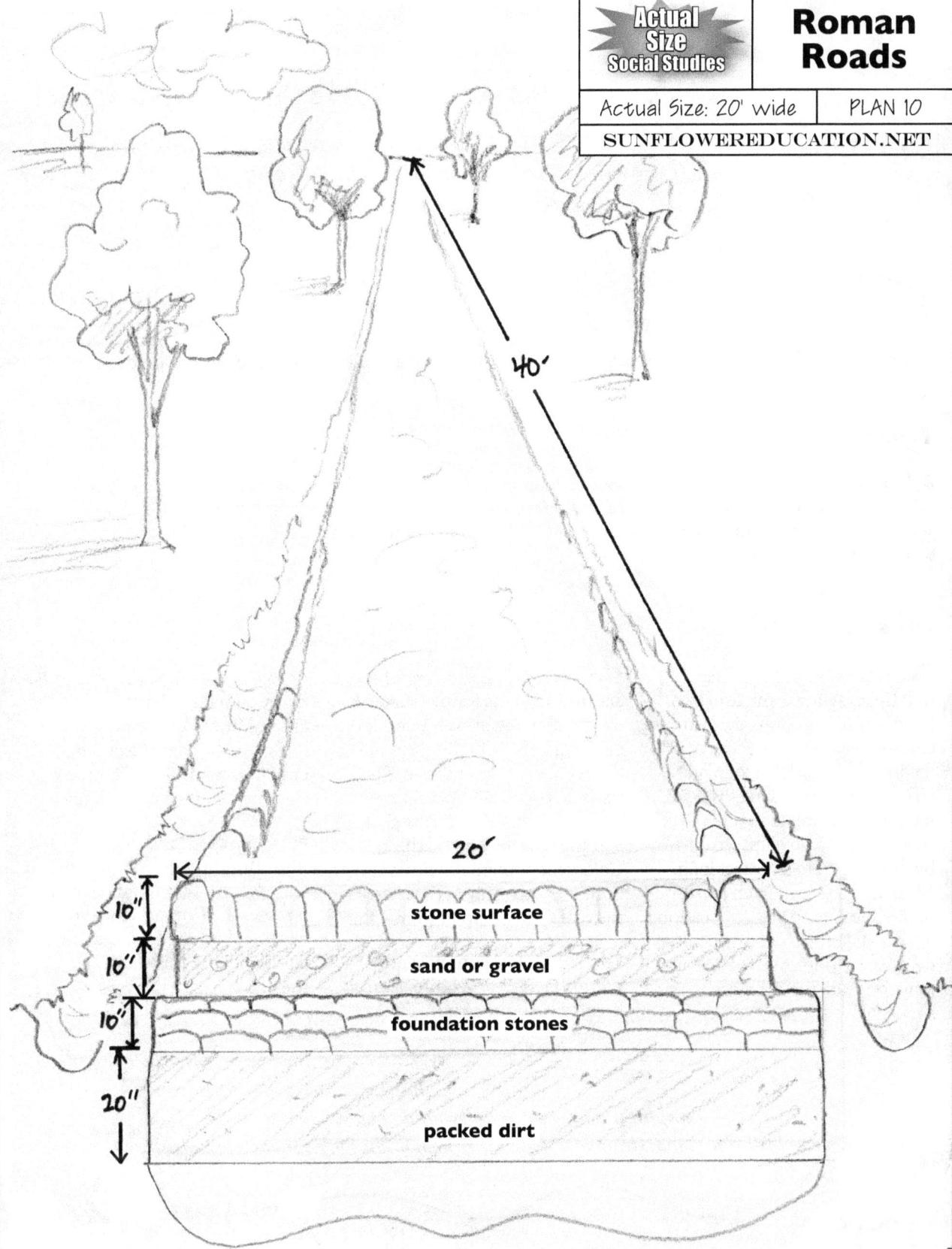

The Roman Colosseum

Students create a scale drawing of the Roman Colosseum in order to visualize this world famous landmark.

Prepare

- *Allow time:* approximately 2 hours for this activity
- *Gather materials:* Plan 11, measuring tape or measuring wheel, chalk, carpenter's square, stakes (2), string

Focus

Ask students when they last went to a live theater. What did they see there—a movie, a play, a concert? What was the theater like? Explain to students that people have been going to theaters for centuries. The kinds of entertainment may differ from age to age, but everybody wants to see a good show! The people who went to the Roman Colosseum were no exception.

Present

❶ Consult Plan 11. Notice that the drawing is made of two large ellipses. To draw the two ellipses, use the "gardener's oval" technique, in which a loop of string around two stakes is held taught as it is walked around the stakes, tracing an ellipse. Begin by drawing a line 155-feet long. Measure 34 feet in from each end of the line. These are the locations for the stakes for the larger, outer oval. Use a loop of string 242-feet long to create the correct size and shape. Now measure 52 feet in

from each end of the line. These are the locations for the stakes for the smaller, inner oval. Use a loop of string 124-feet long to create the correct size and shape. The space between the two ellipses represents audience seating, and the smaller ellipses the Colosseum's floor. As big as this outline is, it is only ¼ the size of the real Colosseum in Rome, Italy!

❷ The Colosseum was an *amphitheater,* or a large, round theater without a roof. The

Romans staged *gladiator* fights, plays, mock sea battles, and animal hunts here. Ask students if they think that these kinds of entertainment are different from the ones that we have today.

❸ Fifty thousand people could fit in the audience of the Roman Colosseum. Out of all of these people, the Roman emperor, or ruler, had the best seat. Ask students why this may have been the case.

--- Vocabulary ---

ellipse: an oval shape

amphitheater: a large and round open-air theater

gladiator: a man trained to fight other men or animals for entertainment

Conclude

Have students draw a circle next to their diagram of the colosseum, which is an ellipse. How is the ellipse different from the circle? How is it similar? Explain that both shapes are curved. If you drew a bunch of lines through the middle of the ellipse, though, they wouldn't all be equal, as they would be in the circle.

128'

155'

34'

54'

70'

45'

54'

34'

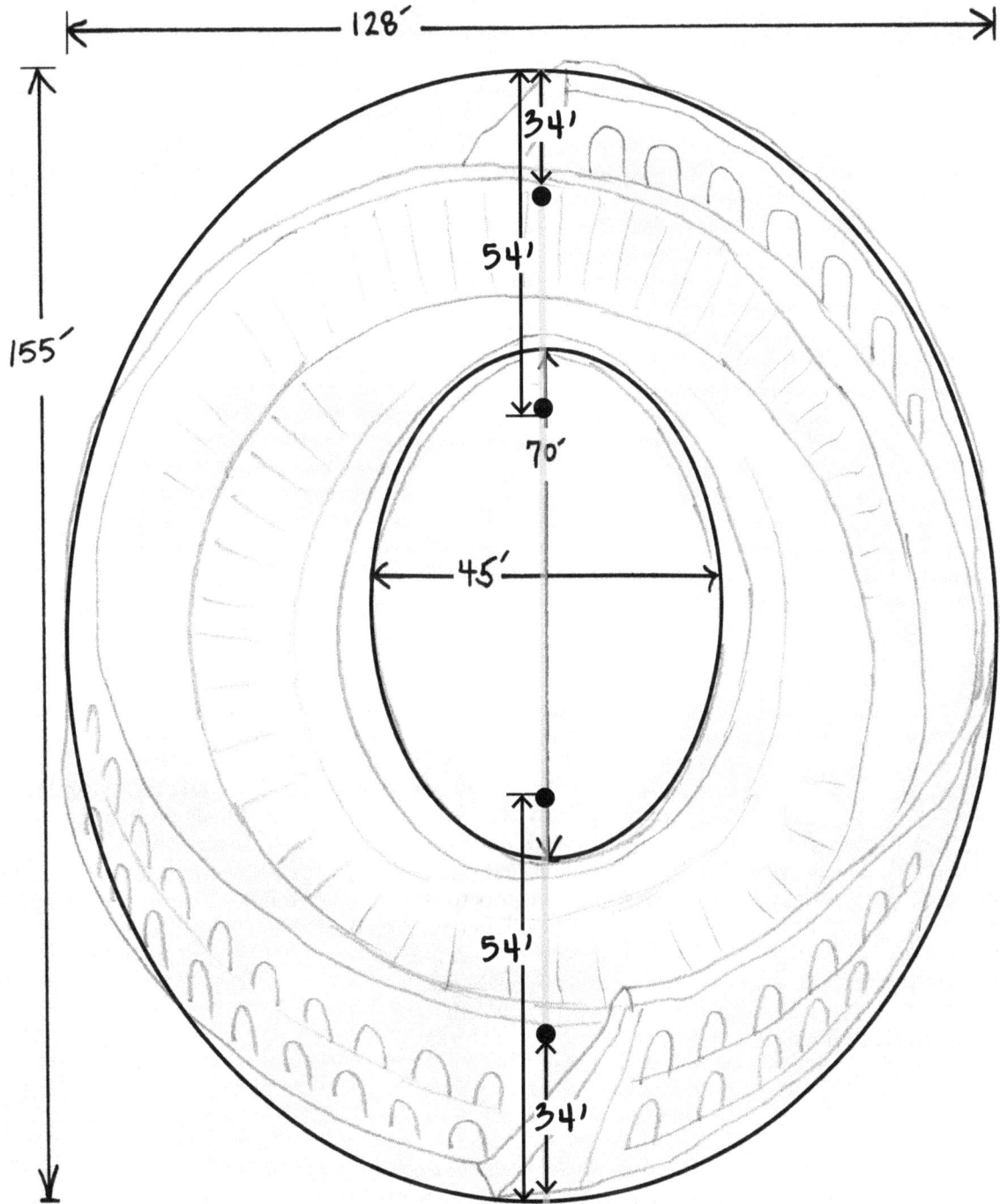

Gardener's Oval

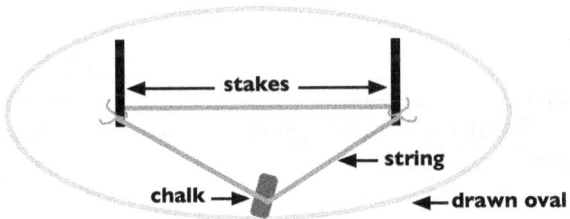

stakes

string

chalk

drawn oval

Actual Size Social Studies

Roman Colosseum

Actual Size: 615' long

PLAN 11

SUNFLOWEREDUCATION.NET

Activity 12

The Great Wall of China

Students create a full-scale cross section of the Great Wall of China in order to visualize this ancient marvel.

Prepare

- *Allow time:* approximately 1 hour for this activity
- *Gather materials:* Plan 12, measuring tape or measuring wheel, sidewalk chalk, chalk line, carpenter's square

Focus

The Great Wall of China is so big that people used to think you could see it from the moon. That isn't actually true, but the whole wall is believed to cover about 5, 500 miles. That's pretty big! Even though it was built a long time ago—starting in the 5th century BCE—it still amazes people all over the world.

Present

❶ Consult Plan 12. On the playground (or appropriate indoor floor), draw a 25-foot line using the measuring wheel and chalk line. This is the base. Draw another 25-foot line perpendicular to the first line using the carpenter's square. Draw a line at the top that is 20 feet long and which does not quite meet the second line. Using the illustration as a template, draw the *cross section* of the wall, with a place for guards or modern-day visitors to stand and walk. The edges of the wall should be 2 feet long and 6 feet tall. Complete the diagram, connecting the two edges of the wall.

❷ Ask students why the Great Wall of China might have been built. Make sure they understand that it was built to protect China from *invasions* by nomads.

———————————————— *Vocabulary* ————————————————

cross section: the view that results when you cut through a three-dimensional object
invasion: when an army or group of people enters a country by force

Conclude

Share pictures of the Great Wall of China with your students. Use your class's new drawing as a visual aid, and ask students to imagine that they are visiting the Great Wall. If time permits, have them make postcards describing their imaginary trip to "send" to family and friends.

Great Wall of China

Actual Size: 25' x 25' | PLAN 12

SUNFLOWEREDUCATION.NET

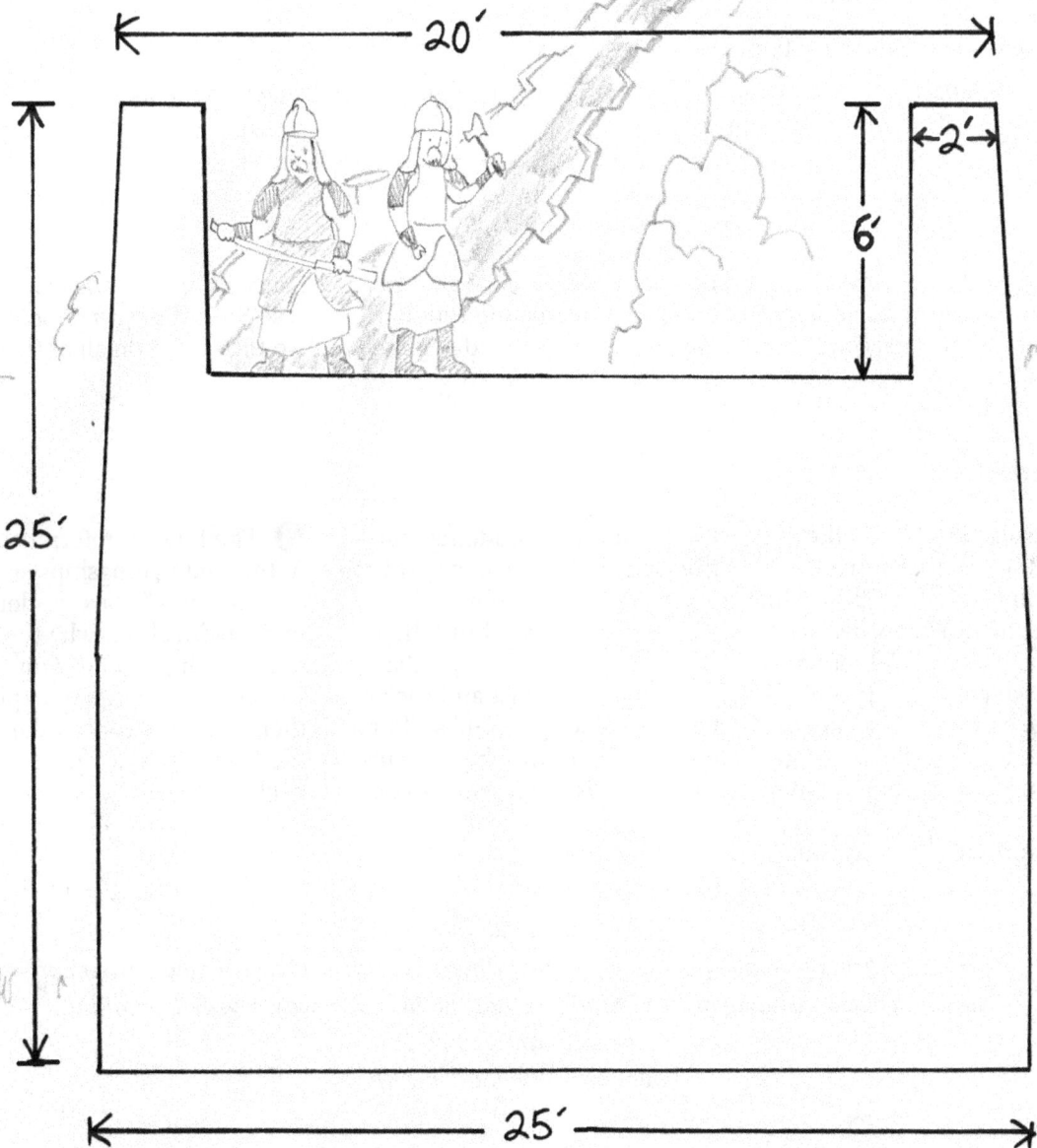

20´

2´

6´

25´

25´

Viking Ship

Students create a full-scale outline of a Viking ship in order to learn about Viking travel and raids.

Prepare

- *Allow time:* approximately 45 minutes for this activity
- *Gather materials:* Plan 13, measuring tape or measuring wheel, sidewalk chalk, chalk line, carpenter's square

Focus

There's a good chance you've heard of Vikings. They have an important place in history because they traveled to many different lands and *colonized* many different places. These *Scandinavian* people were merchants, explorers, conquerors, and pirates. They needed good ships to take them on all of their adventures.

Present

❶ Consult Plan 13. On the playground (or appropriate indoor floor), draw a 70-foot line using the measuring wheel and chalk line. Draw a 15-foot line at a right angle to the first line using the carpenter's square, and complete the rectangle. Using the illustration as a guide, have students draw an outline of a Viking ship, called a "longship."

❷ Point out to students that the longship is much longer than it is wide. Ask them why the Vikings might have built their ships in this way. Explain that it made longships fast and easier to navigate. Vikings could still fit a lot of goods in the ship because it was long without being bulky.

❸ The English referred to the Viking longships as "dragonships." Have students brainstorm about why the shape of a longship would remind someone of a dragon. Explain to them that the front of the ship, or the *bow,* is shaped like a dragon's neck and head.

——————————————— Vocabulary ———————————————

colonize: when a group of people moves to a different land to create a new settlement
Scandinavia: an area of northern Europe that includes Norway, Sweden, Denmark, Finland, and Iceland
bow: the front end of a ship

Conclude

There were several different kinds of longships, each of which were used for different purposes. The smallest were called *Karvi,* and they were used for fishing and trade. The *Snekkja, Skei,* and the *Drekar* were used for warfare. Have students say aloud how they think these names are pronounced and what they think the most exciting part about life as a Viking was.

Actual Size
Social Studies

Viking Ship

Actual Size: 70' long | PLAN 13

SUNFLOWEREDUCATION.NET

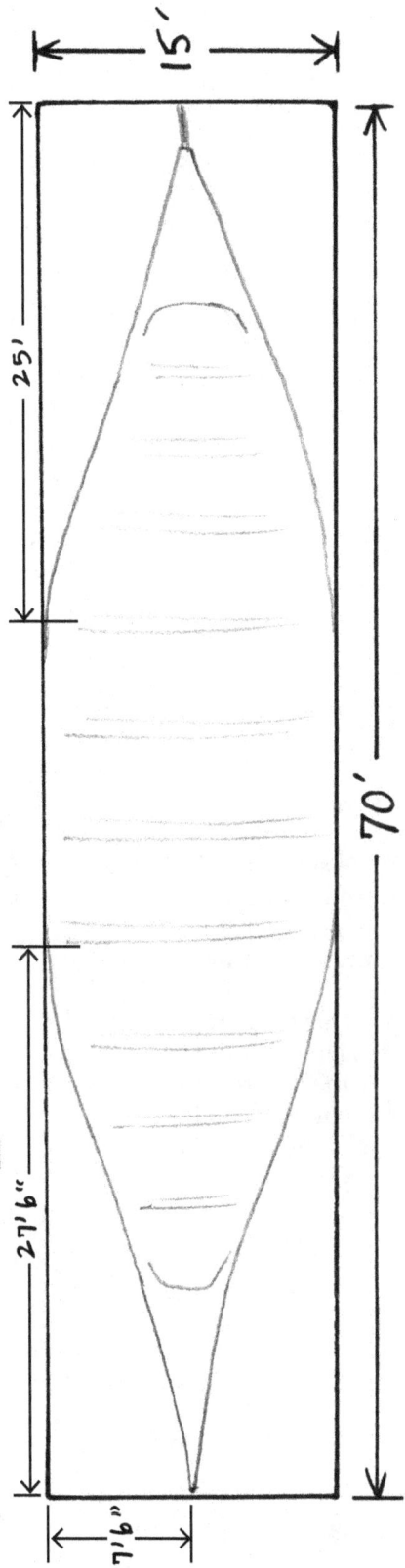

15'

25'

70'

27' 6"

7' 6"

A Medieval Castle

Students create a to-scale drawing of an actual castle in order to visualize life in Medieval Europe.

Prepare

- *Allow time:* approximately 3 hours for this activity
- *Gather materials:* Plan 14, measuring tape or measuring wheel, sidewalk chalk, chalk line, carpenter's square, string, stake

Focus

Ask your students to name their favorite fairy tales. There's a good chance that most of these stories were set in castles, which were huge buildings made of stone. They had towers and were surrounded by *moats*. Perhaps they actually were home to a few enchanted frogs or scary witches, but they usually just housed noblemen and women.

Present

❶ Consult Plan 14. On the playground, draw a rectangle that is 150 feet by 130 feet using the measuring wheel, chalk line, and carpenter's square. This represents the *curtain wall* of the castle. Draw another rectangle inside the first rectangle beginning at the point 20 feet inside of the first rectangle. This second rectangle should be 110 feet wide and 90 feet long.

❷ Have students return to the curtain wall, and erase an area that is 10 feet long in the middle of the top lines of both rectangles to make an "entrance." In front of the entrance, create a "gatehouse" by drawing a 20-foot line perpendicular to the exterior wall, 45 feet from the corner. Draw a 70-foot line at a right angle to the 20-foot line, and then complete the rectangle.

❸ To make the towers of the castle, place a stake at one corner of the castle and tie a 15-foot piece of string to it. Hold the end of the string and, keeping it taught, draw a circle as you walk around the stake in the middle. Repeat at the other three corners. This is an actual-size outline of Bodiam Castle in England!

Vocabulary
---

medieval: from the Middle Ages, c. 500-1500 CE
moat: a deep, wide ditch filled with water that surrounds and protects a castle
curtain wall: a wall that surrounds a castle and usually links towers together

Conclude

If time permits, have students sit inside of the castle and tell them a fairy tale. The story will surely come alive in such an enchanted setting! Ask students what they think life was like as a nobleman or woman.

Actual
Size
Social Studies

Medieval Castle

Actual Size: ~150'square | PLAN 14

SUNFLOWEREDUCATION.NET

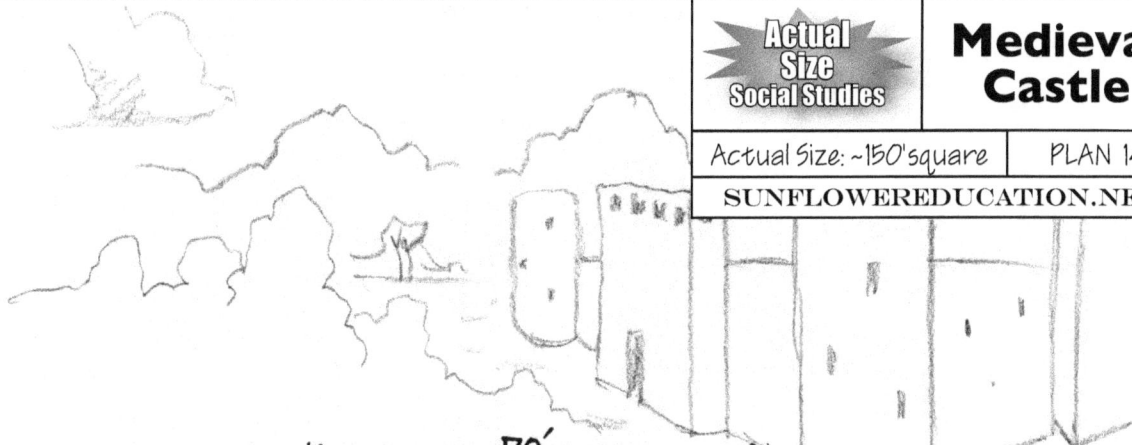

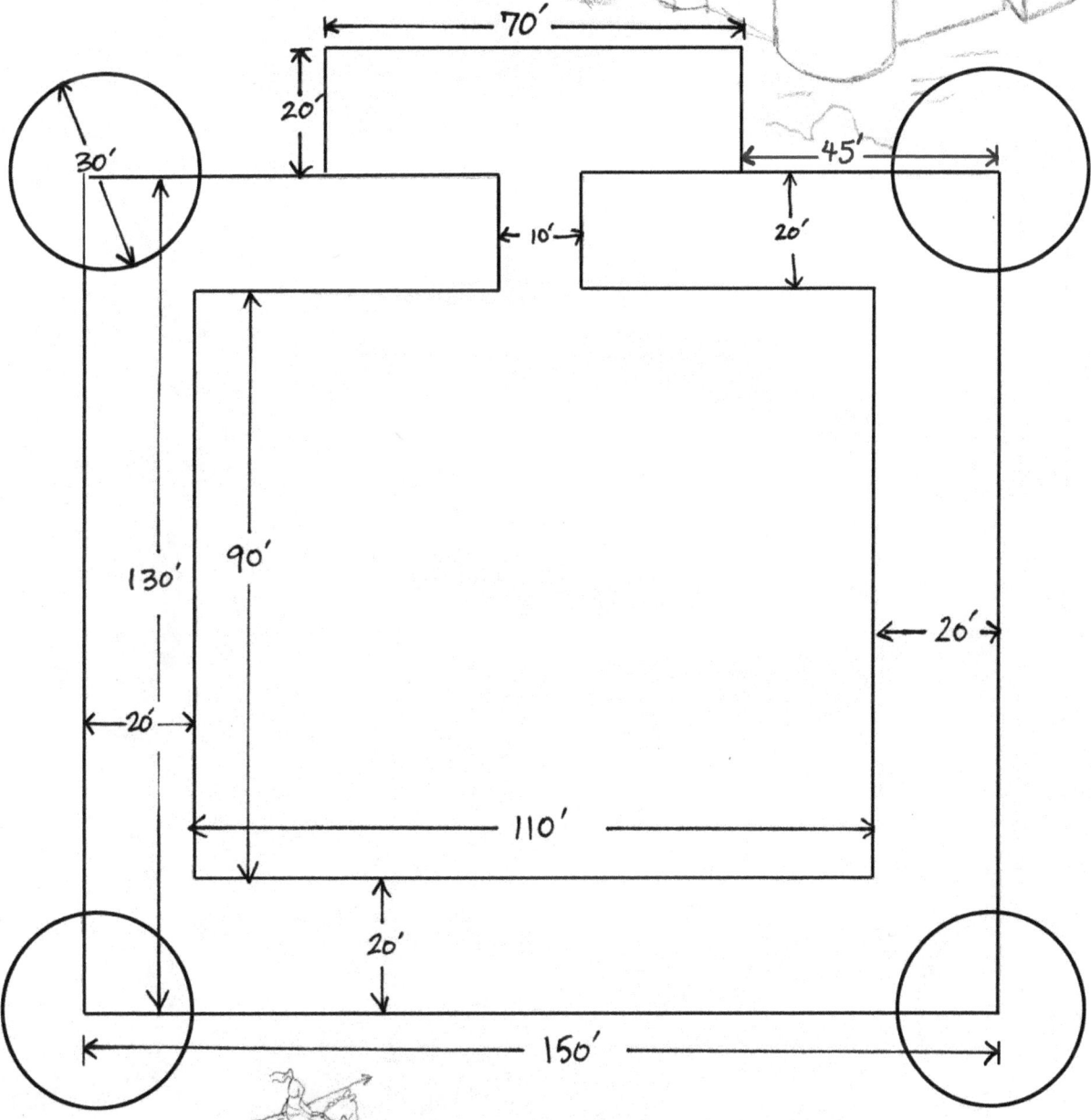

70'

20'

30'

45'

20'

10'

130'

90'

20'

20'

110'

20'

150'

Native America

Activity 15

Native American Boats

Students outline a dugout canoe and a bull boat in order to appreciate the importance of watercraft to Native Americans.

Prepare

- *Allow time:* approximately 45 minutes for this activity
- *Gather materials:* Plan 15, measuring tape, sidewalk chalk, chalk line, carpenter's square, string, stake

Focus

Discuss with students the importance of boats in the modern world. It is likely that most of the toys, furniture, and electronics in their homes that were made in other countries came to America on ships. Explain to students that boats were one of the earliest forms of transportation.

Present

❶ Consult Plan 15. On the playground (or appropriate indoor floor), place a stake in the ground and tie a 3-foot, 6-inch piece of string to it (or have a student stand in one place and hold the string). This is the outline of the bull boat. Draw another circle 4-feet, 6 inches inside of the first circle to differentiate bottom and side of the boat. Next, on another section of the ground, draw a 15-foot line using the measuring wheel and chalk line; draw another, 3-foot line at a right angle to the end of the first line using the carpenter's square. Then complete the rectangle. This is the outline of the dugout canoe.

❷ The name "dugout canoe" tells you how such a boat is made. Dugout canoes are made by taking a large tree and carefully digging out wood from the center so the boat will float and people can ride in it. Some Native Americans on the Pacific coast in the North built dugout canoes that were able to carry 60 people! How many students will fit in the outline of the dugout canoe?

❸ Bull boats were generally smaller than dugout canoes. The *hull* of a bull boat was made from a buffalo *hide*. The Native Americans who built bull boats would make a bowl shape out of tree branches and pull a bull buffalo hide tightly over the outside of this big bowl.

_____ Vocabulary _____

hull: the main body of a ship, including the bottom and sides that touch the water
hide: skin

Conclude

Discuss with students whether it would be easier to travel a long distance in a dugout canoe or a bull boat. Encourage students to spend time inside the outlines and think about the shapes of both boats. Direct students to think about how water would flow around each boat, and then point out that because of its narrower, longer shape, the dugout canoe is much easier to steer and to travel long distances in.

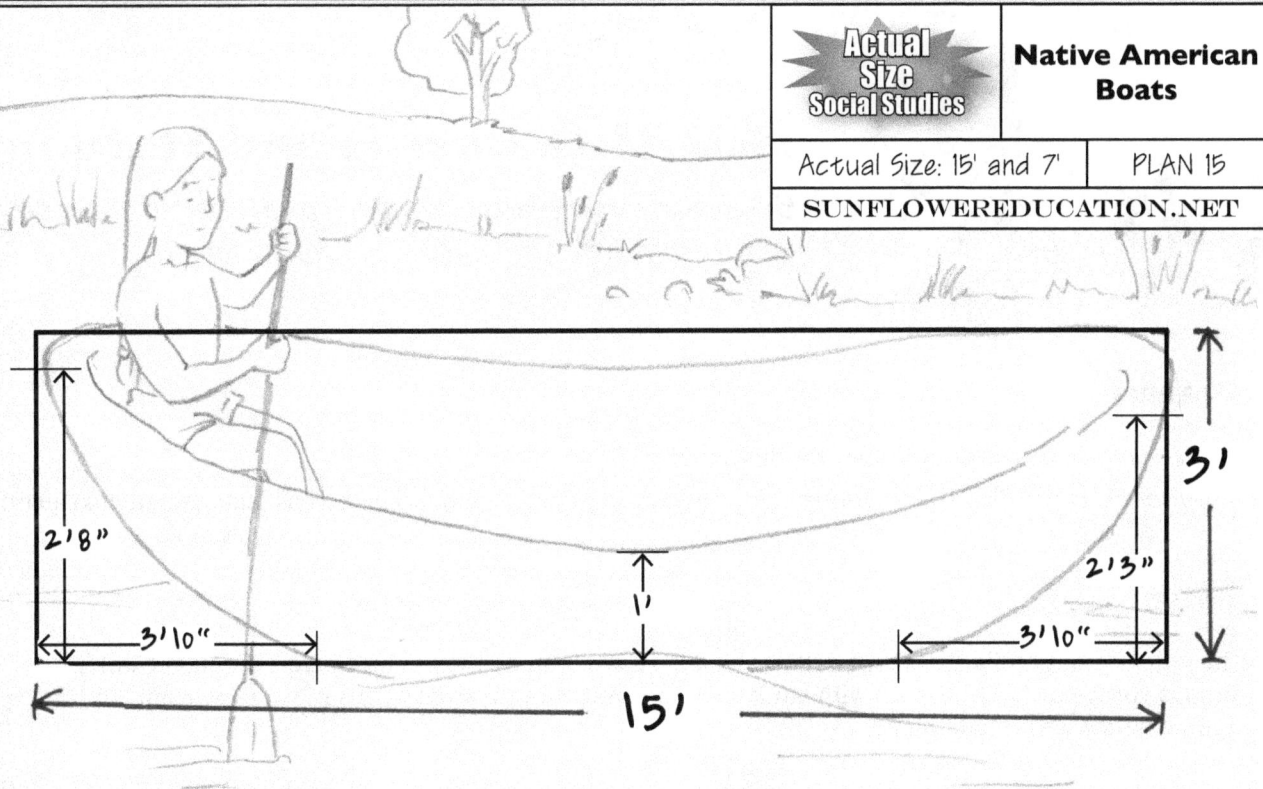

3'

2'8"

2'3"

1'

3'10"

3'10"

15'

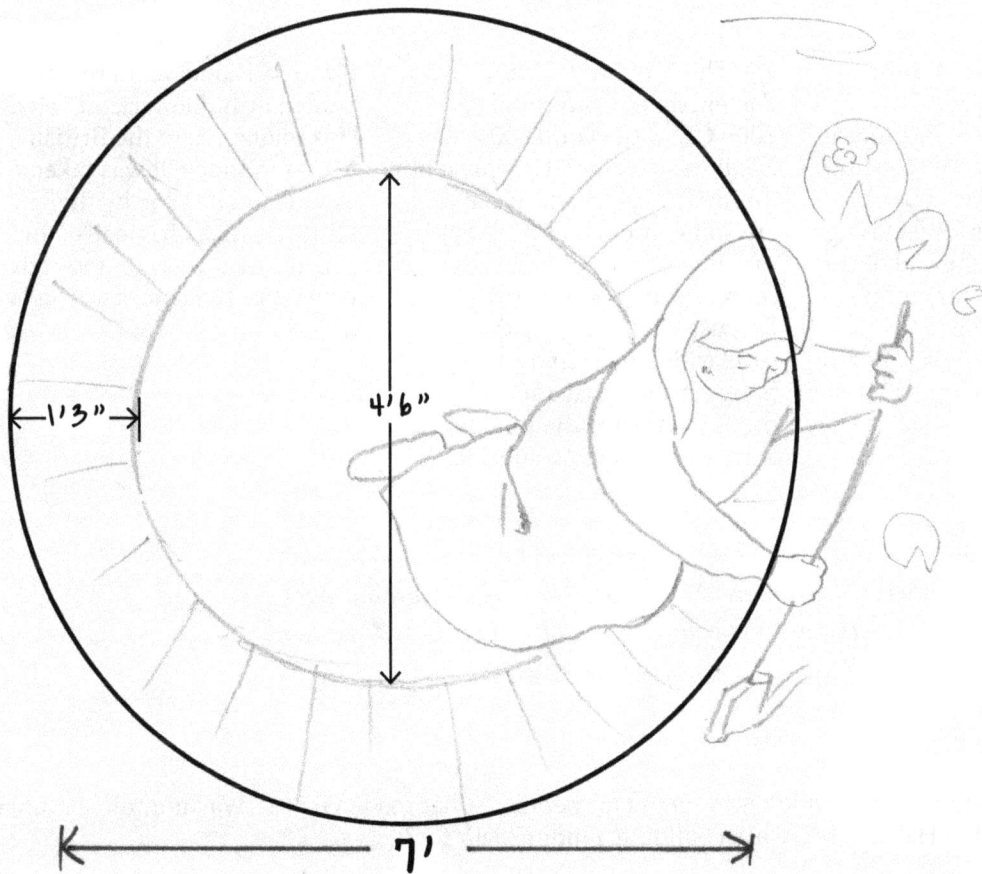

4'6"

1'3"

7'

Moai (Easter Island Statue)

Students outline Hoa Hakananai'a (a Moai) in order to gain insight into the culture of Easter Island.

Prepare

- *Allow time:* approximately 1 hour for this activity
- *Gather materials:* Plan 16, measuring tape or measuring wheel, sidewalk chalk, chalk line, carpenter's square

Focus

The great statues on Easter Island, called Moai, have fascinated visitors since before Captain Cook's famous voyage in 1774. Discuss with students important cultural *monuments* in your town and/or significant national monuments.

Present

❶ Consult Plan 16. On the playground (or appropriate indoor floor), draw a line that is 8 feet long using the measuring wheel and chalk line; draw another line that is 33-feet long at a right angle to the end of the first line using the carpenter's square. Then complete the rectangle. Using the Plan 16 as a template, have students fill in the details of Hoa Hakananai'a inside the rectangle.

❷ The Moai were made on Easter Island from roughly 1000 CE to the late 1600s. The Moai were created to represent important *ancestors*. What are some important national monuments in America that represent important Americans? Discuss with students the similarities and differences between the Moai and monuments like the Lincoln and Washington Memorials.

❸ Hoa Hakananai'a means "stolen or hidden friend." Hoa Hakananai'a is in the British Museum today. It was taken to England in 1868 by the HMS *Topaze*. Originally, Hoa Hakananai'a was painted red and white, but the colors washed off in the sea.

———————————————— Vocabulary ————————————————

monument: *a structure built to commemorate a famous person or event*

ancestor: *someone from whom a person is descended*

Conclude

Discuss with students why we build monuments for people. What made George Washington, Abraham Lincoln, and the Hoa Hakananai'a worth building a monument for?

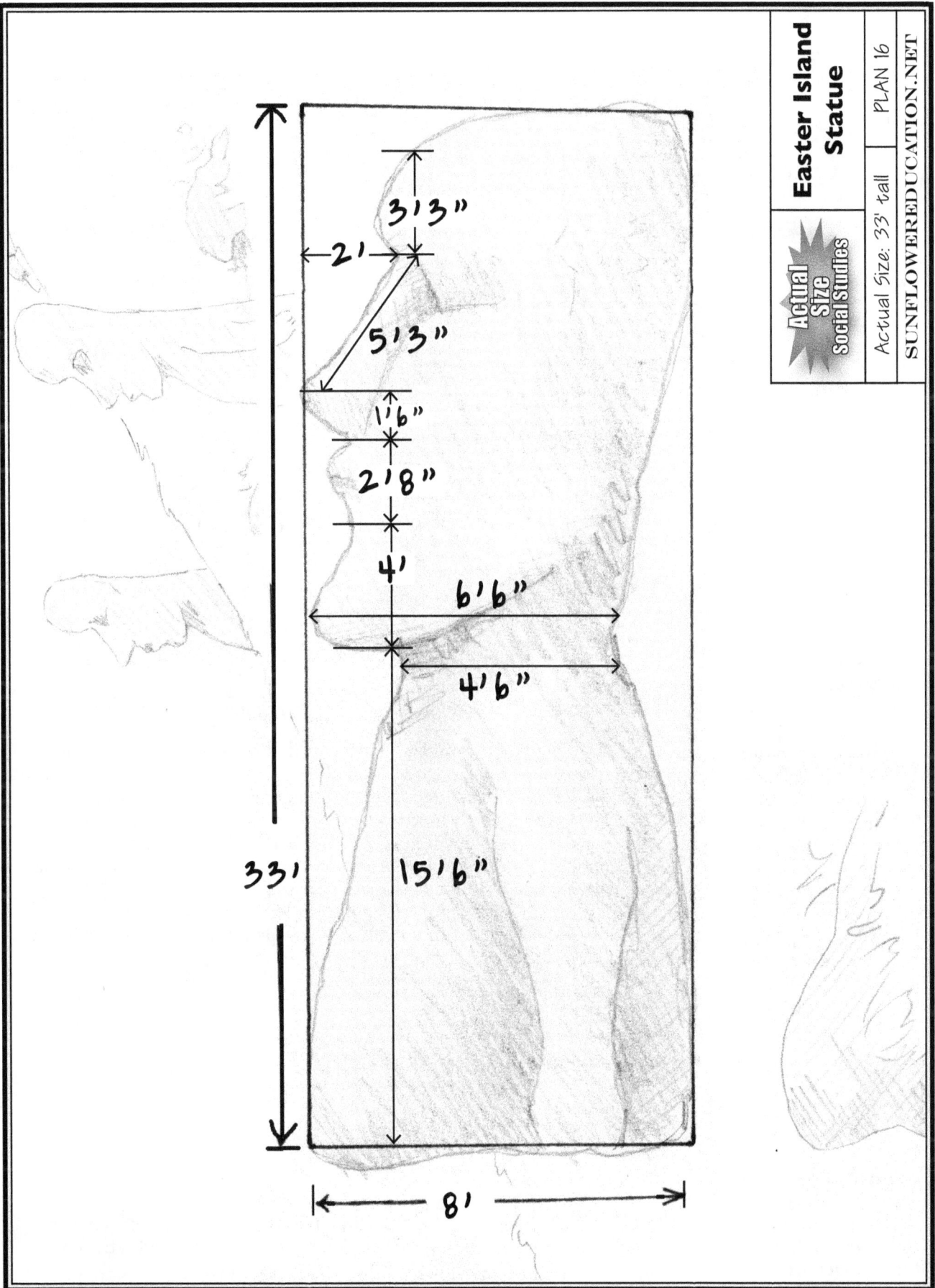

Easter Island Statue

PLAN 16

Actual Size: 33' tall

SUNFLOWEREDUCATION.NET

Actual Size
Social Studies

3'3"

2'

5'3"

1'6"

2'8"

4'

6'6"

4'6"

33'

15'6"

8'

Activity 17
Inuit Igloo

Students outline an igloo in order to appreciate this ingenious Inuit invention.

Prepare

- *Allow time:* approximately 30 minutes for this activity
- *Gather materials:* Plan 17, measuring tape, sidewalk chalk, carpenter's square, string, stake

Focus

People live in a variety of *environments*. For a very long time, the Inuit have lived in some of the coldest and most *inhospitable* environments on Earth. Before heaters and electricity, the Inuit invented a building that could be built quickly on hunting trips to keep them warm.

Present

❶ Consult Plan 17. On the playground (or appropriate indoor floor), place a stake in the ground and tie a 3-foot piece of string to it (or have a student stand in one place and hold the string). Hold the end of the string and, keeping the string taught, draw a circle as you walk around the stake in the middle. From the edge of the circle, draw a 4-foot line using the measuring tape and chalk line; draw another 3-foot line at a right angle to the end of the first line using the carpenter's square. Then complete the rectangle.

❷ Contrary to popular belief, igloos were not the permanent homes of most Inuit people. Igloos were mostly built on hunting trips. The Inuit went further North to hunt seals and other animals. In the far North far less *vegetation* grows than in the rest of the world, so the Inuit eat a lot more meat than people in most other places. These igloos kept the Inuit warm in inhospitable environments.

❸ Have students spend time in the igloo outline. There is not a lot of space inside. Discuss with students why the Inuit would want to stay in such a small space. (It's easier to warm a small space). The inside of an igloo can be 40 degrees higher than the temperature outside of the igloo!

─────────── Vocabulary ───────────
environment: the type of place in which one lives
inhospitable: not friendly or welcoming
vegetation: plants

Conclude

Many people often think of the word Eskimo instead of Inuit. Eskimo is a word that outsiders came up with for the Native American people of the far North. Inuit means "the people" in Inuit and is the name they prefer. Discuss why it is important to refer to people by the name that they prefer.

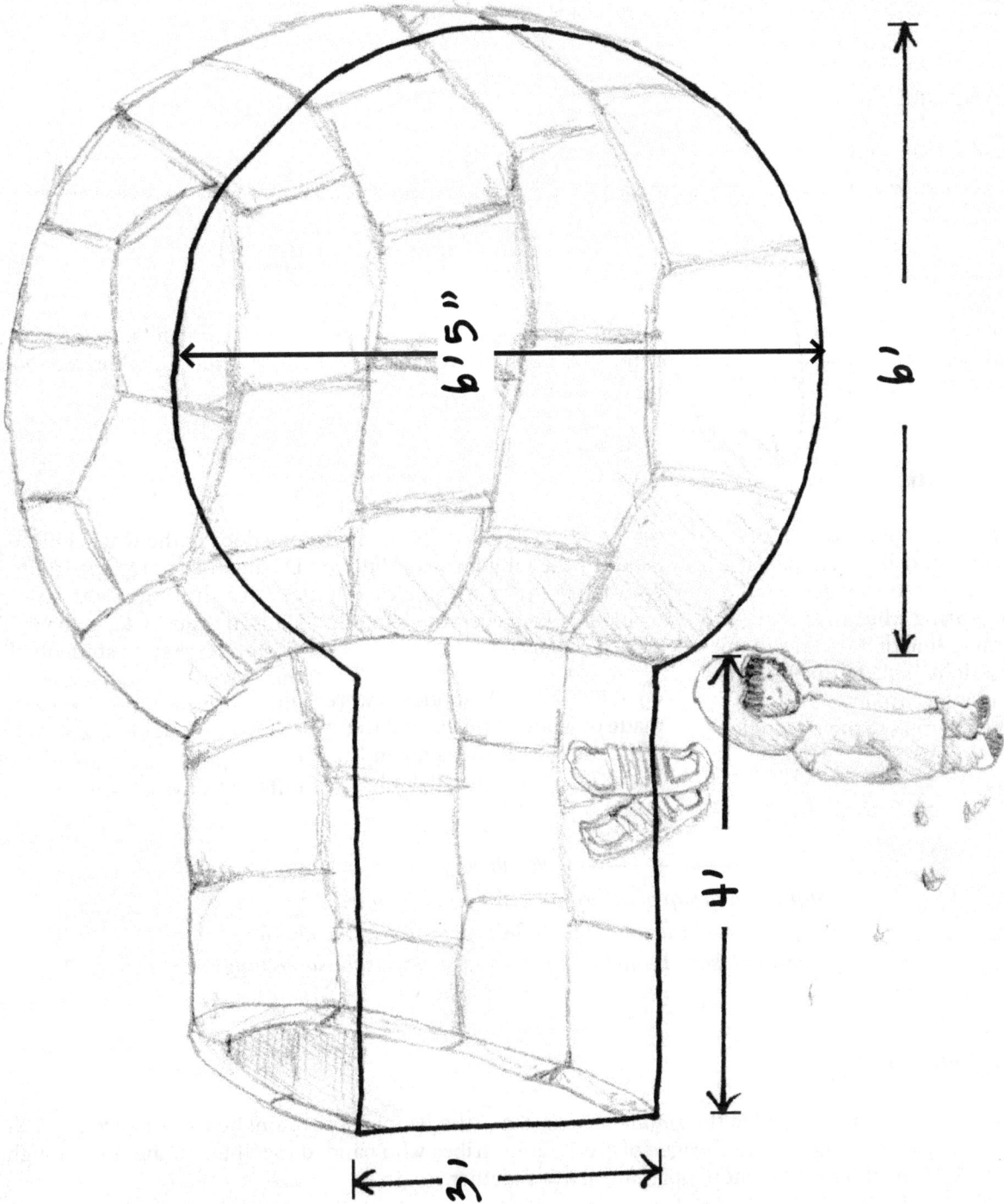

6'5"

6'

4'

3'

Iroquois Longhouse

Students create a to-scale drawing of an Iroquois Longhouse in order to learn about how these Native Americans lived.

Prepare

- *Allow time:* approximately 45 minutes for this activity
- *Gather materials:* Plan 18, measuring tape or measuring wheel, sidewalk chalk, chalk line, carpenter's square

Focus

Ask students how many families usually live in a house or apartment. For most students, the answer will be one. Then, tell students that 20 or more families all lived together in an *Iroquois* Longhouse. Good thing it was a long building!

Present

❶ Consult Plan 18. On the playground, draw a line that is 180-feet long using the measuring wheel and chalk line. Draw a line that is 20 feet long at a right angle to the first line using the carpenter's square. Then complete the rectangle.

❷ Have the whole class sit inside of the longhouse outline. Now tell them to imagine what it would be like if everyone's family were there, too!

❸ The walls of longhouses were made of wooden poles, and the roofs were made of leaves and grass. There was usually only

one door in the whole building! During the winter, the Iroquois covered the house with animal skins in order to keep the cold air out. Explain to students that this method of building is very different from the ones we use today, but it worked well for the Iroquois. There are many different ways to build houses!

――――――――― Vocabulary ―――――――――

Iroquois: A group of different Native American tribes who lived in the northeastern United States and parts of Canada

symbol: something that represents or stands for something else

Conclude

The Iroquois were also called the *Haudenosaunee,* or, "the People of the Longhouse." The Iroquois were not just one tribe. They were a league of six different tribes who banded together. To them, the longhouse was a *symbol* of how different people can all live together.

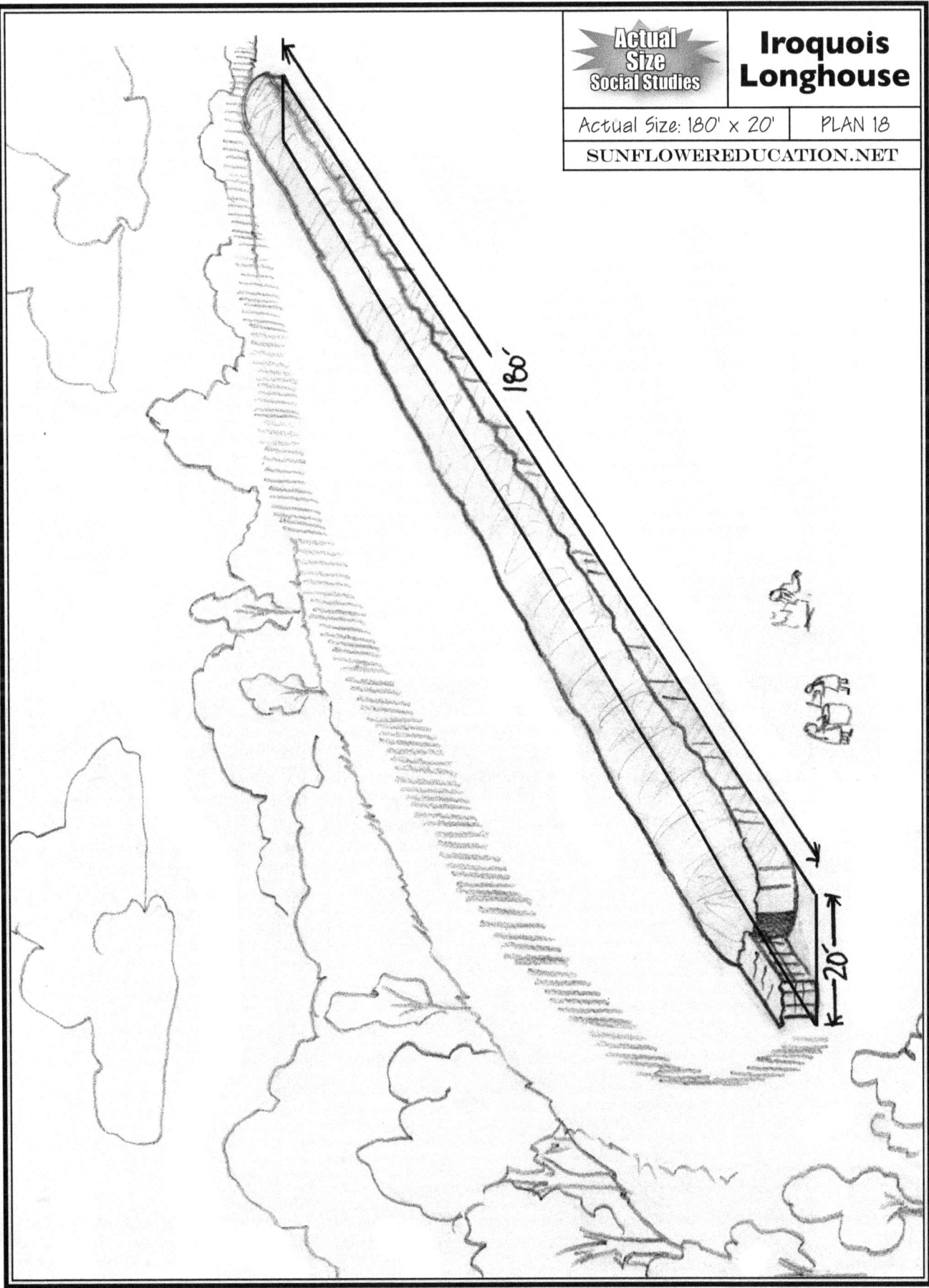

180'

20'

Sioux Tipi

Students outline a Sioux tipi in order to gain insight into the Sioux way of life.

Prepare

- *Allow time:* approximately 30 minutes for this activity
- *Gather materials:* Plan 19, measuring tape or measuring wheel, sidewalk chalk, string, stake

Focus

Have any of your students ever moved from one house to another? Imagine if they could have brought their old house with them! Many Native Americans, including the *Sioux* (pronounced "sue") lived in tipis. Tipis were houses that could be broken down and rebuilt. The Sioux were *nomads*. They had to move around to hunt, and so they needed movable houses.

Present

❶ Consult Plan 19. On the playground (or appropriate indoor floor), place a stake in the ground and tie a 7 ½-foot piece of string to it (or have a student stand in one place and hold the string). Hold the end of the string and keeping the string taught, draw a circle as you walk around the stake in the middle.

❷ Have students sit inside the tipi outline. How many can comfortably fit? Explain how important the buffalo were to Plains Indians. They were sources of food, clothing, fuel (dung), tools and even homes—the hides were used for the tipi walls.

❸ What would it be like to be a Sioux for a day? What might students do inside of a tipi? Explain to them that they might tell stories or paint a picture on a buffalo hide. They might have built a fire in the tipi, and the smoke would leave the tipi through a hole in the top of the tipi. They might have ate, slept, laughed, did chores—just like everybody else.

───────────────── Vocabulary ─────────────────

Sioux: A Native American tribe that originally lived in the Western and Midwestern United States
nomads: a group of people who don't have a fixed home
sign language: a way of communicating to someone by using movements of the hands and arms

Conclude

Here's a cool fact: the Sioux traded with other tribes who lived in the Great Plains. These other tribes did not always speak the same language, so the Sioux and the other tribes created a *sign language* that everyone in the area could understand.

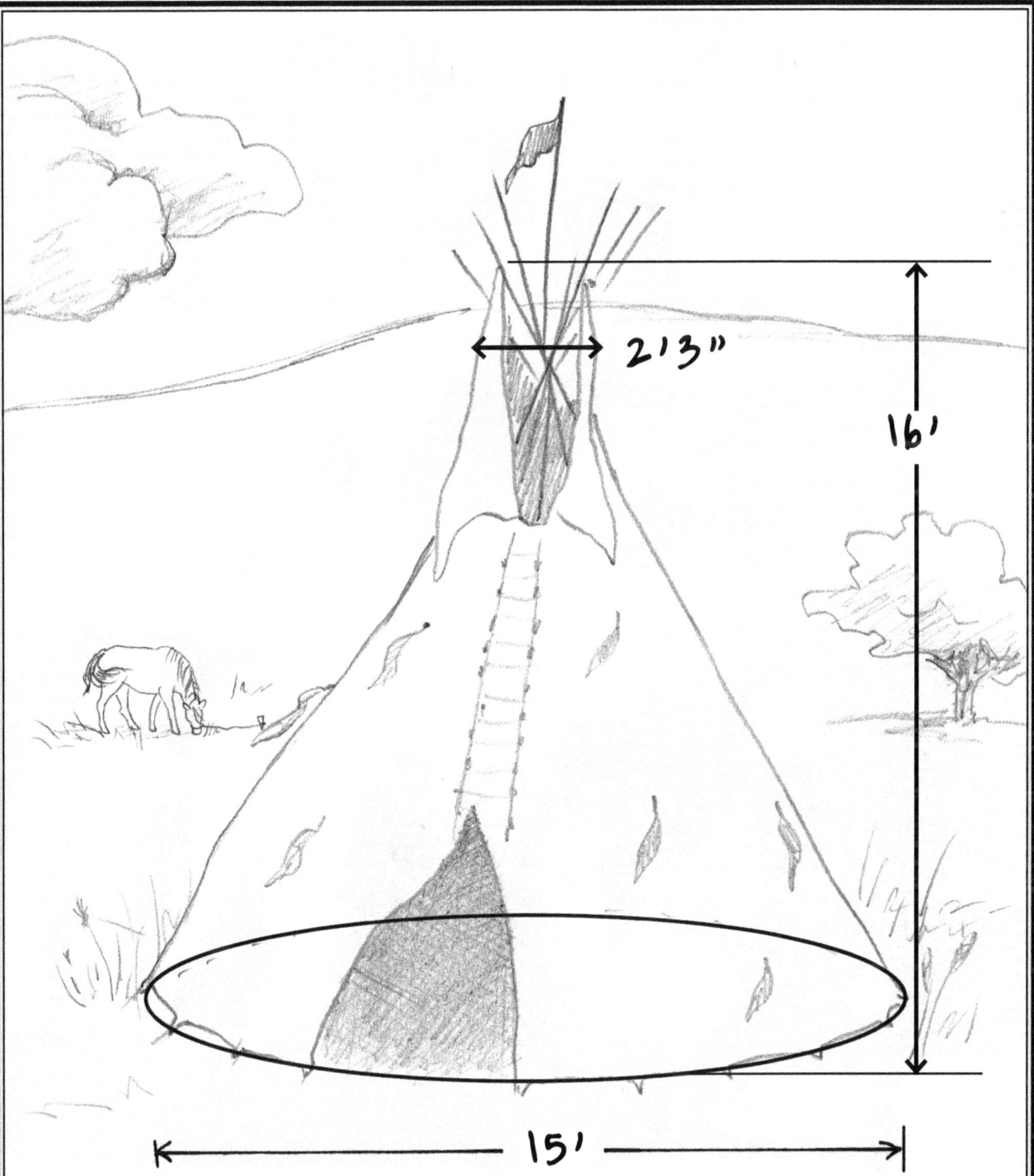

2'3"

16'

15'

Actual Size Social Studies

Sioux Tipi

Actual Size: 15' wide	PLAN 19

SUNFLOWEREDUCATION.NET

U.S. History

Log Cabin

Students outline a log cabin in order to understand what it was like to live on the American frontier.

Prepare

- *Allow time:* approximately 30 minutes for this activity
- *Gather materials:* Plan 20, measuring stick or measuring wheel, sidewalk chalk, chalk line, carpenter's square

Focus

The *pioneers* who settled on the American *frontier* had to build their own homes. Discuss with students what it would have been like to leave your home and travel to a whole new part of the country where you would have to build a new house. Discuss with students what houses are made of and explain that on the frontier, trees were often the best material people had to make houses out of.

Present

❶ Consult Plan 20. On the playground (or appropriate indoor floor), draw a line that is 16 feet long using the measuring wheel and chalk line; draw another line that is 16 feet long at a right angle to the end of the first line using the carpenter's square. Then complete the square.

❷ Discuss with students what it takes to build a log cabin. After picking out the trees and cutting them down, people would notch the ends so that all four walls of the cabin would be snugly connected to one another. After stacking the logs for the walls, any gaps between the logs had to be filled in with *chinking*, a flexible material made of moss and clay, to keep out rain, cold, heat, and bugs.

❸ Have students spend time in the log cabin. Discuss with students what kinds of things would be in the log cabin: a fireplace, a table, chairs, a bed, and maybe a desk or bookshelf. Use chalk to outline items on the floor. Have students imagine living with their whole family in this log cabin.

―――――――――――――― Vocabulary ――――――――――――――

pioneer: one of the first people to settle in a new place
frontier: the edge of settled territory

Conclude

Several of America's former presidents were born and grew up in log cabins. Abraham Lincoln was born in a log cabin. Discuss with students why President Lincoln may have talked about being born in a log cabin. He did this to show that he understood normal people and wasn't someone born into riches.

16' -

16'

Activity 21
Conestoga Wagon

Students outline a Conestoga wagon in order to see how far commercial transportation has come.

Prepare

- *Allow time:* approximately 30 minutes for this activity
- *Gather materials:* Plan 21, measuring stick or measuring wheel, sidewalk chalk, chalk line, carpenter's square

Focus

Today, people transport *goods* all across the country in boats, trains, airplanes, and trucks. Back in the 17 and 1800s though, most of these options weren't available. Discuss with students the importance of water *transportation,* and then talk about the necessity of land transportation. Before train tracks crossed America, goods had to be transported in animal-drawn wagons across land. One of the most effective of these was the Conestoga wagon.

Present

1 Consult Plan 21. On the playground (or appropriate indoor floor), draw a 17-foot line using the measuring wheel and chalk line; draw another 4-foot line at a right angle to the end of the first line using the carpenter's square. Then complete the rectangle. Tell students the height of Conestoga wagon measuring from the bottom of the wheels to the top of the canvas was 11 feet. Point to that height on a wall.

2 People and goods traveled over large distances in these wagons. Have students place their backpacks, chairs, and other items in the wagon, and imagine taking a 100-mile trip in the wagon. As the Conestoga wagon typically covered about 15 miles per day, this 100-mile trip would take almost 7 full days!

3 Conestoga wagons carried very large amounts of cargo. Many of them could carry as much as 8 tons! These wagons were pulled by horses or oxen. It would not have been uncommon to see 6-8 horses or up to 12 oxen pulling a Conestoga wagon.

Vocabulary ---
goods: items that have value
transportation: a way of getting from one place to another
commercial: having to do with commerce or trade

Conclude

Discuss with students how far *commercial* transportation has come. What means do we use today to transport goods? Planes, trains, trucks, ships, et al. Discuss with students what kinds of transported goods are the same today as they were in the 1700s and 1800s. What are some different ones?

Actual
Size
Social Studies

Conestoga Wagon

Actual Size: 17' x 4' | PLAN 21

SUNFLOWEREDUCATION.NET

4'

17'

Prairie Schooner

Students outline a prairie schooner in order to recreate the journey of American settlers traveling West.

Prepare

- *Allow time:* approximately 30 minutes for this activity
- *Gather materials:* Plan 22, measuring stick or measuring wheel, sidewalk chalk, chalk line, carpenter's square

Focus

Today when people move across the country, they usually move all of their possessions by car, truck, or trailer. Early American pioneers did not have these options. They took themselves and all of their belongings west in prairie *schooners*.

Present

❶ Consult Plan 22. On the playground (or appropriate indoor floor), draw a line that is 11 feet long using the measuring wheel and chalk line; draw another line that is 4 feet long at a right angle to the end of the first line using the carpenter's square. Then complete the rectangle. This is an outline of a prairie schooner from above.

❷ A prairie schooner was usually a simple farm wagon with a cover—a "covered wagon." Families would take everything they could all the way across America in these small wagons. Discuss with students what a trip across America in a prairie schooner would be like. How much would students ride and how much would they walk?

❸ Families could only take as much with them as they could fit into their prairie schooner. Much of the space also was needed for food and supplies. Discuss with students what would be important for them to take on such a long move.

—————————— Vocabulary ——————————

schooner: a type of sailboat
fleet: a group of ships

Conclude

People described all of the covered wagons moving West across the plains as looking like a *fleet* of ships on the ocean. The white covers of all these covered wagons resembled sails on ships—hence the famous nickname, prairie schooner.

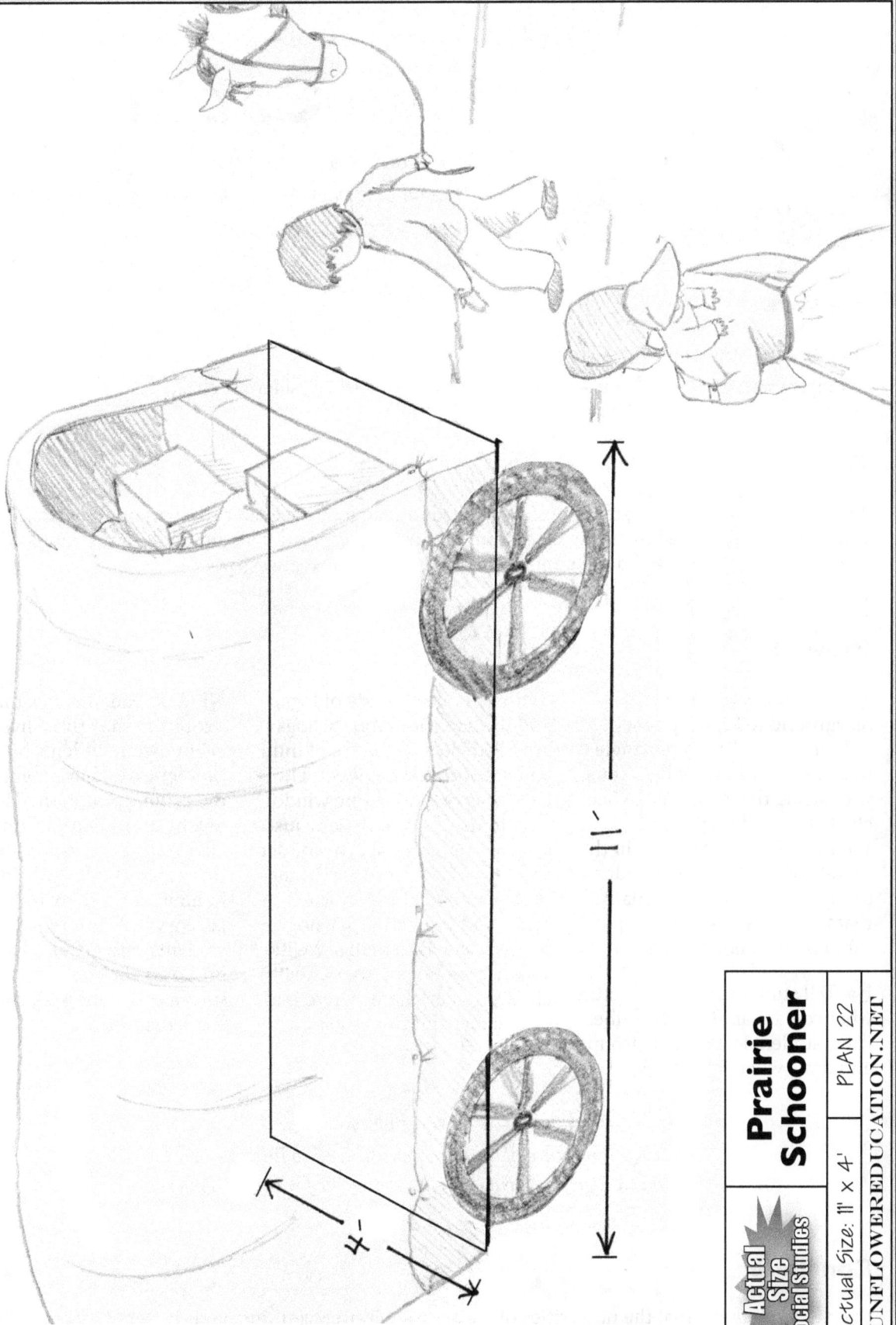

Prairie Schooner

Actual Size: 11' x 4'   PLAN 22

SUNFLOWEREDUCATION.NET

11'

4'

Slave Cabin

Students outline a cabin built by enslaved Africans to appreciate the poor housing and living conditions that they were forced to endure.

Prepare

- *Allow time:* approximately 45 minutes for this activity
- *Gather materials:* Plan 23, measuring tape or measuring wheel, sidewalk chalk, chalk line, carpenter's square

Focus

Remind students of the existence of slavery in American history. Lead a discussion on what they think life as a slave was like. Then focus the discussion on housing. Explain that, although slaves' living conditions varied in different times and different places, they were almost always poor.

Present

❶ Consult Plan 23. On the playground (or appropriate indoor floor), draw a rectangle that is 16 feet long and 14 feet wide using the measuring wheel, chalk line, and carpenter's square. Leave a 2-foot gap in the middle of one of the long sides to represent the door. Explain that this was the size of a typical cabin built to house slaves.

❷ Tell students to try to picture what you are about to describe. Have students break into groups and draw what you describe. The cabin is made of made of logs, and the gaps between the logs are filled with a mixture of mud and straw called *chinking*. The cabin has one door, one window next to the door (not glass; just a square opening with a wooden shutter), and a dirt floor. In the middle of one of the shorter sides is a fireplace. Opposite the fireplace is a small *loft* with a ladder leading up to it. Small children sleep there. There is a small table and two stools and some cooking equipment.

❸ Ask students how many people do they think lived in this cabin. After students have made their guesses, have them enter the cabin through the "door" one by one. Continue until 16 children have entered. Explain that cabins typically held two families, with as many as 16 parents and children. Break the students into groups. Have each group go about a daily activity, such as cooking or sleeping, at the same time.

_____ *Vocabulary* _____

chinking: a mixture of mud and straw used to fill gaps in a log cabin
loft: a high platform used for storage or for extra living space

Conclude

Explain to students that the necessities of life are food, water, clothing, and shelter. Based on what they have learned about the shelter provided for enslaved African Americans, what can they predict about the nature of the food, water, and clothing they had?

Actual
Size
Social Studies

**Slave
Cabin**

Actual Size: 16' x 14' | PLAN 23

SUNFLOWEREDUCATION.NET

14'

16'

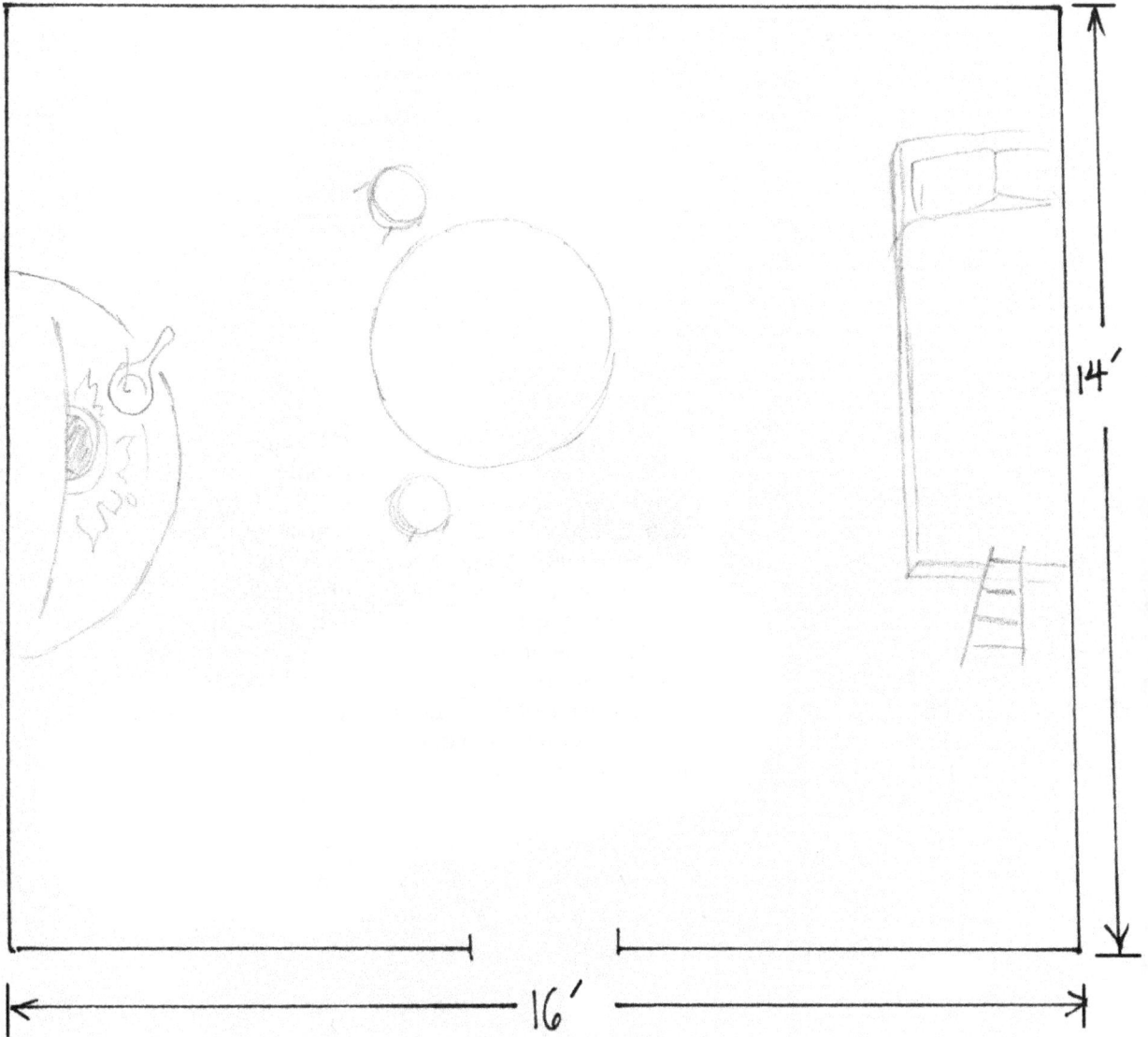

One-Room Schoolhouse

Students outline a one-room schoolhouse in order to understand what school used to be like in America.

Prepare

- *Allow time:* approximately 45 minutes for this activity
- *Gather materials:* Plan 24, measuring stick or measuring wheel, sidewalk chalk, chalk line, carpenter's square

Focus

Discuss with students how big schools are today. Many *elementary* schools throughout the country teach just the first few grades and have hundreds of students. Then explain to students that 150 years ago many schools all over America were just one room—for all the grades!

Present

❶ Consult Plan 24. On the playground (or appropriate indoor floor), draw a line that is 30 feet long using the measuring wheel and chalk line; draw another line that is 22 feet long at a right angle to the end of the first line using the carpenter's square. Then complete the rectangle. This is an outline of a one-room schoolhouse in Minot, Maine.

❷ For a very long time one-room schoolhouses were the norm for most of the people who went to school in America. One teacher taught grades 1-8, and all of these grades were in the same room together. Discuss with students the pros and cons of going to school in a one-room schoolhouse. One of the biggest adventures was that the older children could help the younger children.

❸ 150 years ago, not very many people made it through eighth grade. Many students went to school for the first few years learning reading, writing, and *arithmetic,* and then stopped going to school. Discuss with students why so many more students dropped out of school at such a young age.

———————————— *Vocabulary* ————————————

elementary: a school that teaches the first few grades
arithmetic: addition, subtraction, multiplication, and division
prairie: an area of land covered in grass

Conclude

Many well-known Americans went to school in one-room schoolhouses. Laura Ingalls Wilder, for example, wrote about growing up on the frontier in the *Little House on the Prairie* series. In this series, Laura writes about being both a student and later a teacher.

One-Room
Schoolhouse

Actual
Size
Social Studies

Actual Size: 30' x 22' | PLAN 24
SUNFLOWEREDUCATION.NET

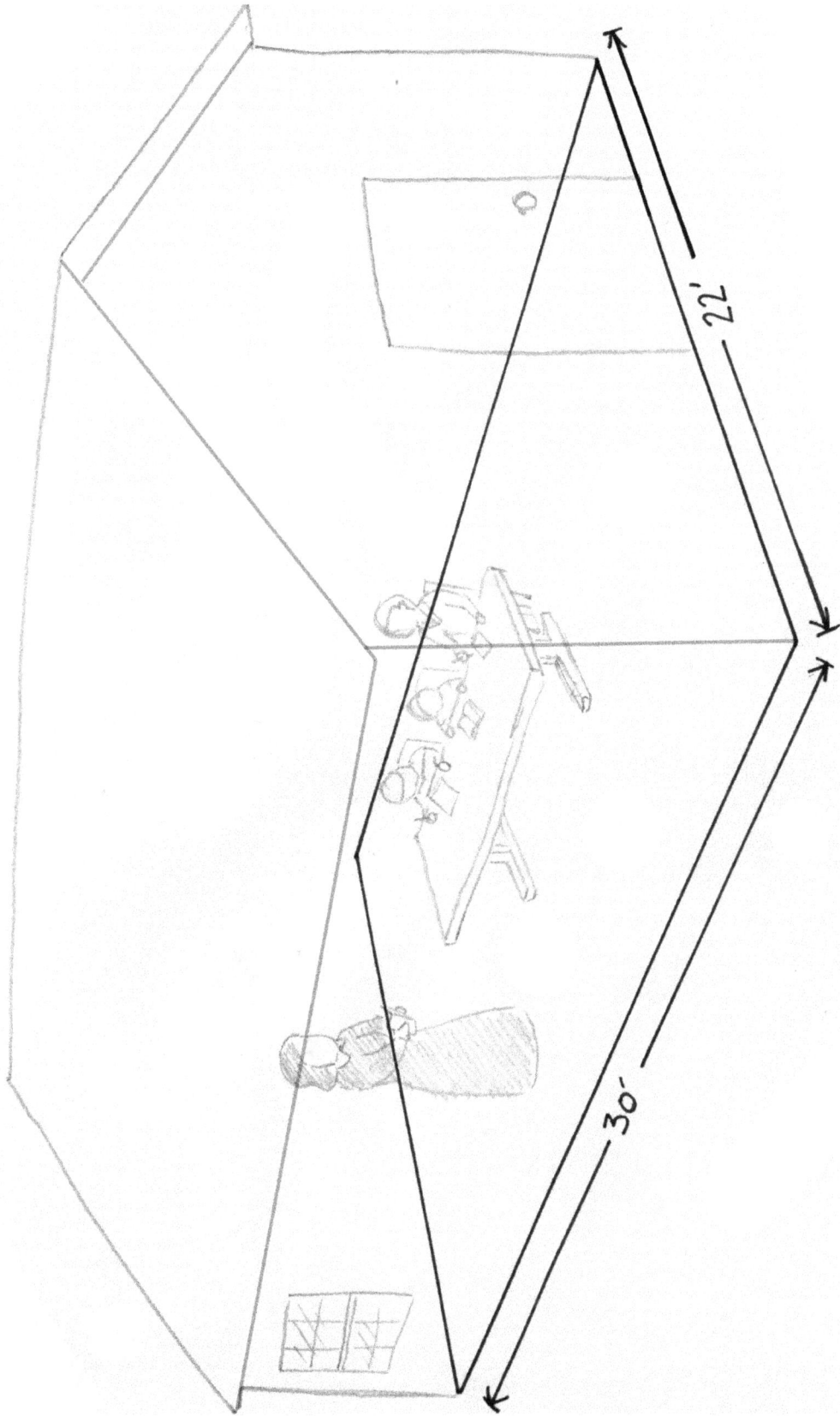

22'

30'

Historic Transportation

The *Santa Maria*

Students outline the Santa Maria in order to help visualize Christopher Columbus's historic first voyage to America.

Prepare

- *Allow time:* approximately 1 hour for this activity
- *Gather materials:* Plan 25, measuring stick or measuring wheel, sidewalk chalk, chalk line, carpenter's square

Focus

Christopher Columbus is one of the world's most famous explorers. He is credited with discovering the Americas. Discuss with students why people *explore.*

Present

❶ Consult Plan 25. On the playground (or appropriate indoor floor), draw a 98-foot line using the measuring wheel and chalk line; draw another, 26-foot line at a right angle to the end of the first line using the carpenter's square. Then complete the rectangle. Using Plan 25 as a guide, have students draw the outline of the *Santa Maria* inside the rectangle.

❷ Explain to students that in 1492, Christopher Columbus set off with three ships to find a new way to get to India. Instead, he came upon North America. Discuss with students what it must have been like to set sail on the ocean, not knowing what you would find. The *Santa Maria* was the smallest of the three ships in Columbus's fleet. She carried 40 men.

❸ Sailors on long journeys at this time would often suffer from a disease called *scurvy.* It was not until centuries later that people discovered that scurvy was caused by not consuming enough vitamin C. British sailors were later known as "limeys" because of the lime juice they would take to sea to safeguard against scurvy.

——————— Vocabulary ———————

explore: to look for something or somewhere new
scurvy: a disease caused by not getting enough vitamin C, often suffered by early sailors

Conclude

Christopher Columbus is often credited with discovering the Americas. An important thing to remember, though, is that there were already whole civilizations of people in the Americas who knew exactly where they were. Christopher Columbus was in charge of the journey that alerted Europe to the existence of the Americas, but he was not the first person to know about the Americas. But his discovery led to European colonization of the Americas, and to the existence of the United States!

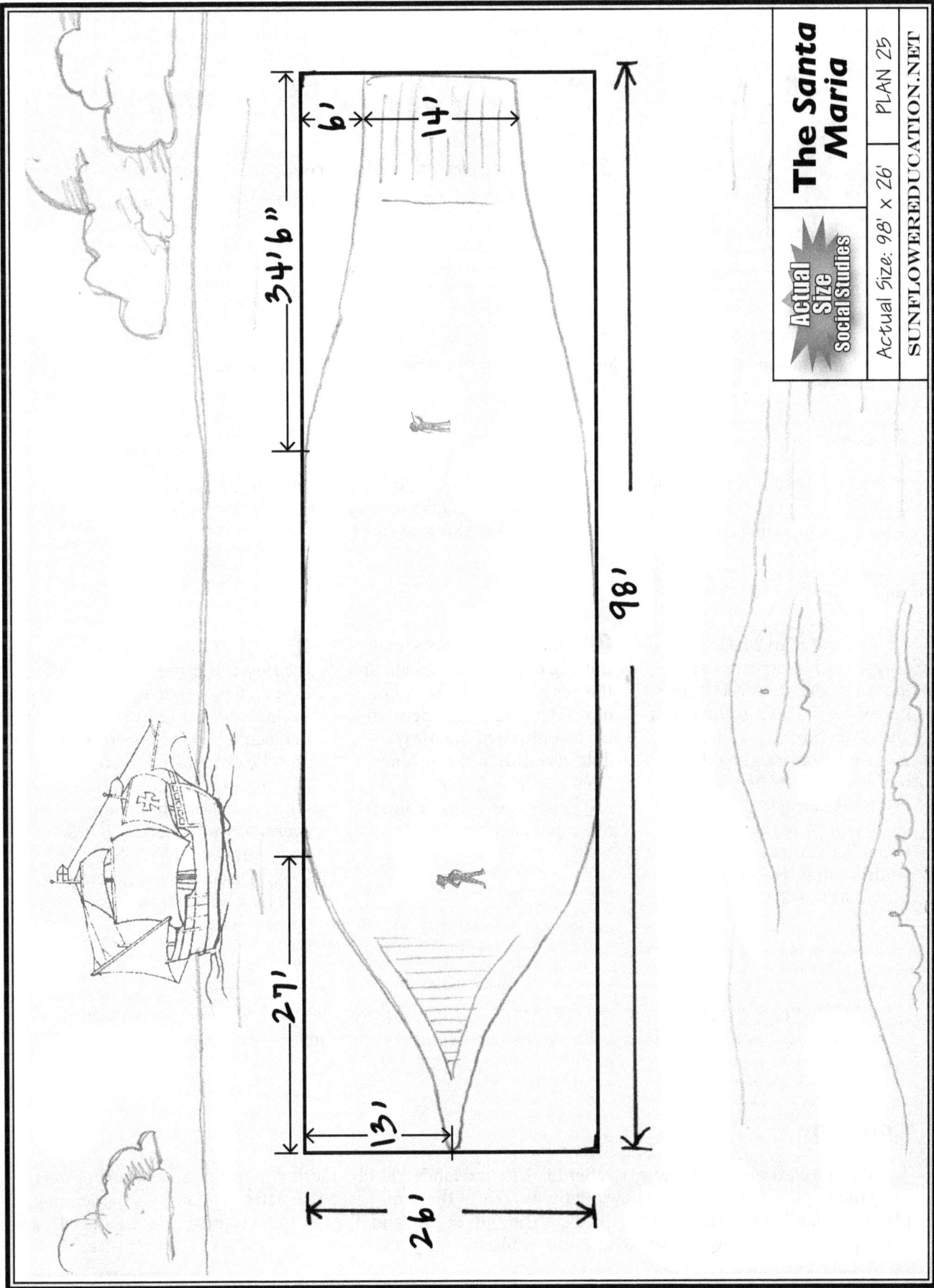

The Santa Maria

Actual Size

Social Studies

Actual Size: 98' x 26'   PLAN 25

SUNFLOWEREDUCATION.NET

9'

14'

34' 6"

98'

27'

13'

26'

The Mayflower

Students outline the Mayflower in order to help visualize the journey of the Pilgrims to America.

Prepare

- *Allow time:* approximately 45 minutes for this activity
- *Gather materials:* Plan 26, measuring tape or measuring wheel, sidewalk chalk, chalk line, carpenter's square

Focus

Today people can fly across the ocean in a matter of hours. Just a few hundred years ago, however, crossing the ocean was a dangerous voyage that would take months. Discuss with students what a flight in an airplane is like compared with a several month-long voyage in a ship.

Present

❶ Consult Plan 26. On the playground (or appropriate indoor floor), draw a 110-foot line using the measuring wheel and chalk line; draw another, 25-foot line at a right angle to the end of the first line using the carpenter's square. Then complete the rectangle. Using Plan 26 as a guide, have students draw the outline of the *Mayflower* inside the rectangle.

❷ Around 130 people made the journey to America aboard the *Mayflower*. The trip took 66 days. Have students spend time in the outline of the *Mayflower*. Talk about what it must have been like to spend 66 days in this space with more than 100 other people.

❸ Explain to students that the *Pilgrims* came to America in search of *religious freedom*. In England, the Puritans were persecuted by the government and the established church because of what they believed. For this reason, they came eventually to America so they could practice their religion freely. Discuss with students the religious freedom we have in the United States.

─────────────── *Vocabulary* ───────────────

Pilgrims: a group of people who left Europe on the Mayflower *in search of religious freedom*
religious freedom: the freedom for people or communities to practice the religion they choose

Conclude

The Pilgrims left Plymouth in September of 1620 and landed at Plymouth in November of the same year. They didn't go in a big circle, so how did they arrive at the same place they left? The Pilgrims named the place they landed in America after the place they left in England, Plymouth. Discuss with students why so many places in America are named after other places.

The Mayflower

Actual Size Social Studies

Actual Size: 110' x 25'

PLAN 26

SUNFLOWEREDUCATION.NET

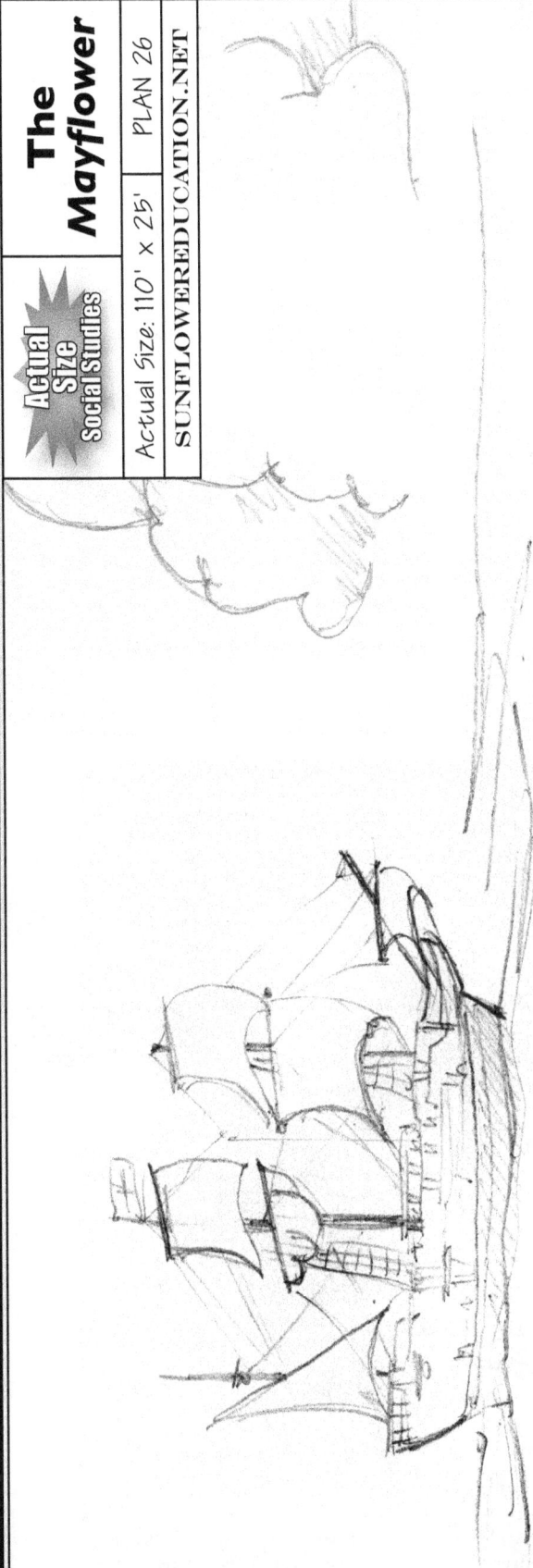

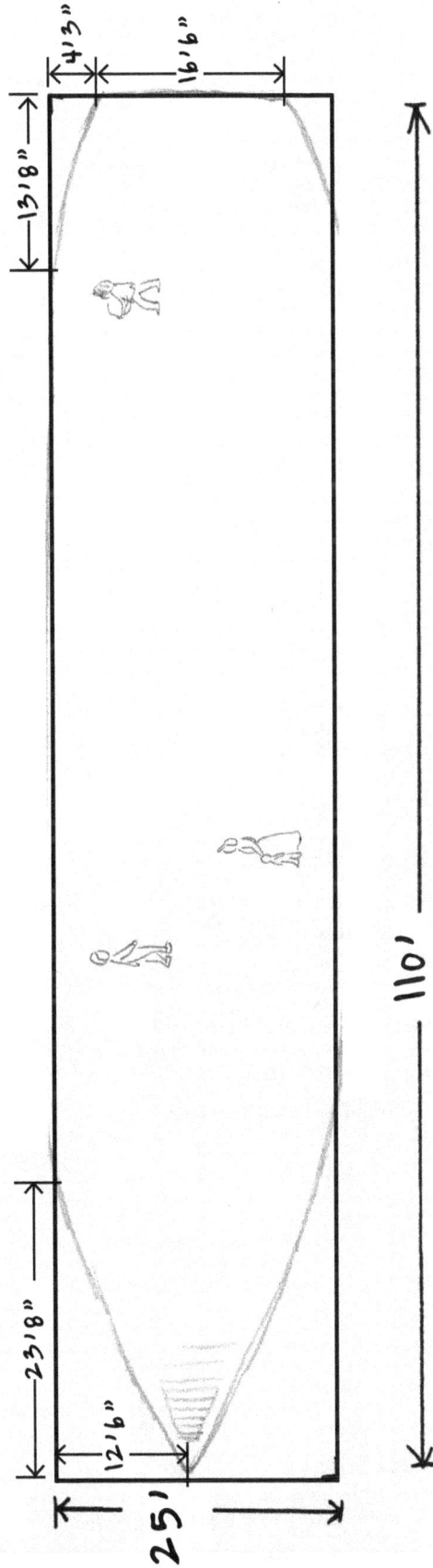

4'3"

9'6"

13'8"

110'

23'8"

12'6"

25'

© 2013 Sunflower Education

Activity 27
The Clermont

Students outline the Clermont in order to learn about the first viable commercial steamboat.

Prepare

- *Allow time:* approximately 1 hour for this activity
- *Gather materials:* Plan 27, measuring tape or measuring wheel, sidewalk chalk, chalk line, carpenter's square

Focus

Imagine a ship that could be mistaken as a sea monster. That is what some people thought the *Clermont* looked like on its first voyage. The *Clermont* was a little funny-looking. It had paddle wheels, sails, and a *smokestack*. It must have looked like it was built from a couple different kinds of ships.

Present

❶ Consult Plan 27. On the playground (or appropriate indoor floor), draw a 150-foot line using the measuring wheel and chalk line. Draw a 13-foot line at a right angle to the first one using the carpenter's square. Complete the rectangle. This represents a view of the *Clermont* from the top. On the 150-foot line, measure in and mark 82 ½ feet. Draw a 4-foot line perpendicular from this point. On each side of this line, draw a 7 ½ foot line, connecting them to the large rectangle. These represent the paddle wheels.

❷ The *Clermont* was a steamship, meaning its *engine* ran off of steam. It wasn't the first ship that was built like that, but it was the first one that could make money by transporting people.

❸ Ask students why the *Clermont* was such an important ship. The fact that it could sail successfully between two cities in New York State meant that other steamships would soon be able to cover longer distances, like along the *Mississippi River*. More people could travel to different places and trade with people in different states.

--- Vocabulary ---

smokestack: a chimney that removes smoke from a locomotive or ship
engine: a machine that changes energy into motion
Mississippi River: a very large American river

Conclude

On its first voyage, in 1807, the *Clermont* sailed from New York City to Albany, New York, covering a distance of 150 miles along the Hudson River. It took 32 hours to get to Albany, with the ship sailing at about 5 miles per hour. Even though the *Clermont* would seem slow to us today, it passed all the other ships sailing on the river.

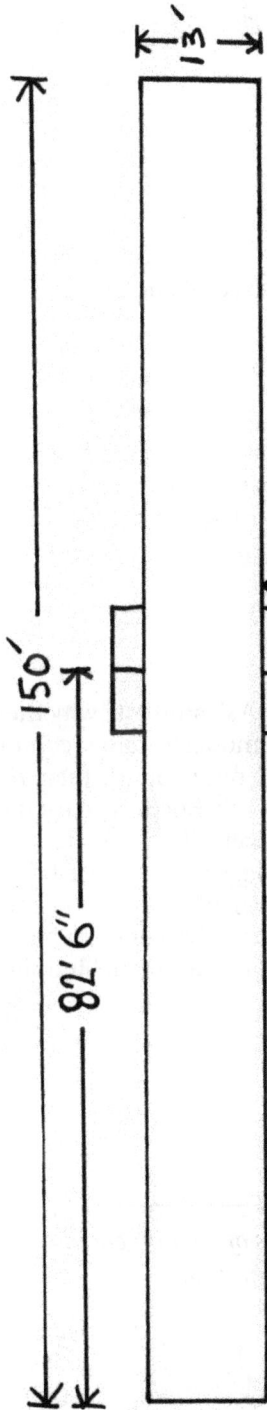

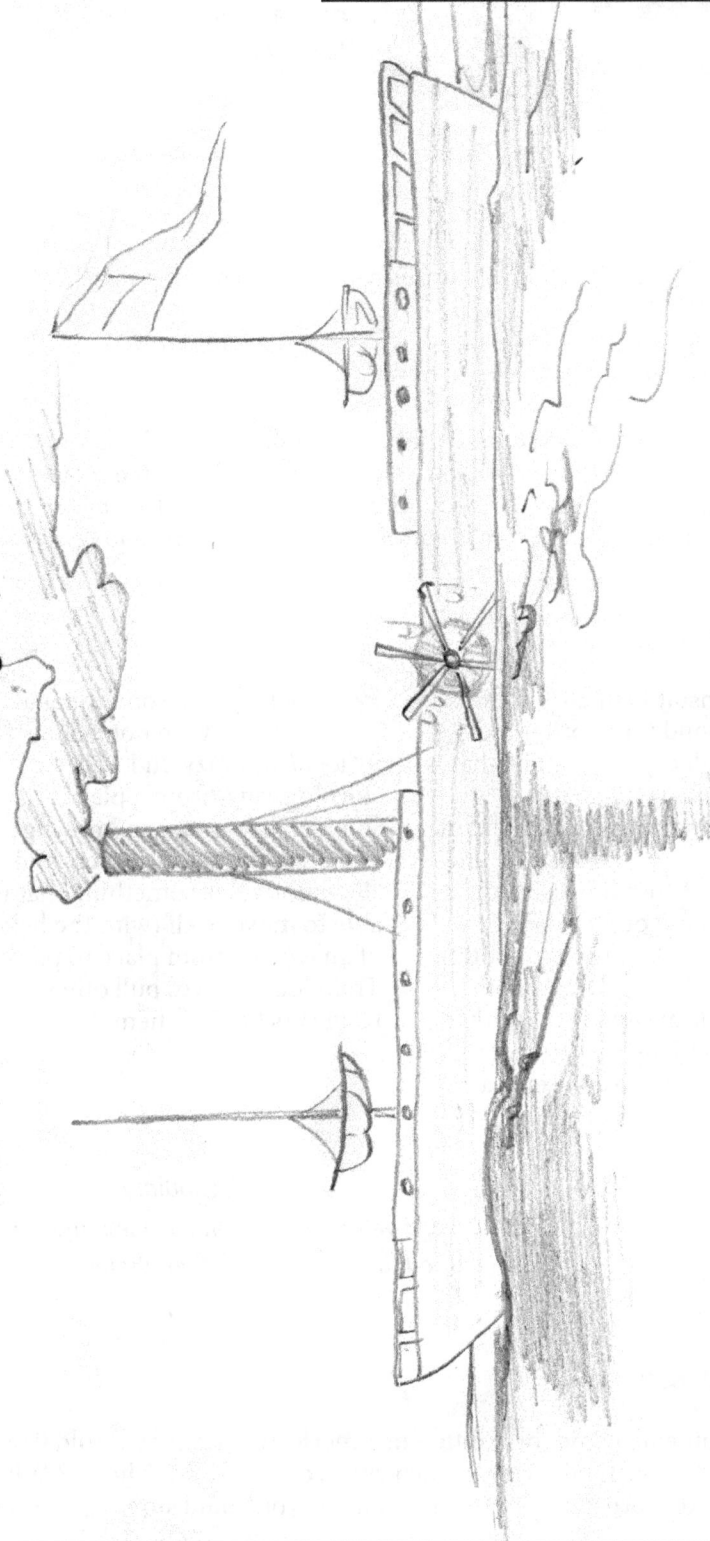

Actual Size Social Studies

The Clermont

| Actual Size: 150' x 13' | PLAN 27 |

SUNFLOWEREDUCATION.NET

Locomotives, Then and Now

Students outline the first American steam locomotive and a modern locomotive in order to see how far trains have come.

Prepare

- *Allow time:* approximately 45 minutes for this activity
- *Gather materials:* Plan 28, measuring tape or measuring wheel, sidewalk chalk, chalk line, carpenter's square

Focus

Which is faster, a train or a horse? Most students would answer "a train," and they would be right. The first steam *locomotive, Tom Thumb,* was challenged to a race with a horse-drawn carriage. At first, *Tom Thumb* was sure to win, but then it broke down. The problem was later fixed and *Tom Thumb* went on to win many races against horses. Trains have come a long way since then!

Present

❶ Consult Plan 28. On the playground (or appropriate indoor floor), draw a line that is 6 ½ feet long using the measuring wheel and chalk line. At right angles to the first line, draw a 13-foot line using the carpenter's square. Complete the rectangle. This is an outline of *Tom Thumb.* Draw another rectangle around the first that is 70-feet long and 10-feet wide. This rectangle represents a modern-day locomotive.

❷ When we call something a "locomotive," we're not calling it "loco," or crazy. In Latin, "loco" means "from a place," so locomotion means "moving from one place to another," and a "locomotive" is something that is able to move itself (with the help of an *engine*) from place to place. Train locomotives pull other train cars behind them.

❸ Ask students why they think the modern train locomotive is so much bigger than *Tom Thumb.* Encourage thoughtful answers. The modern locomotive is bigger because we have more powerful engines and because locomotives need to be able to pull more cars behind them.

─────── *Vocabulary* ───────

locomotive: a vehicle able to move itself and other parts of a train; engine
engine: a machine that changes energy into motion

Conclude

Have students name three different American cities they would like to travel to on a train. Show students a map of the United States. Which city is closest to your home? Which one is furthest away? Are there any two that are in the same direction (i.e. you could stop in one on the way to the other)?

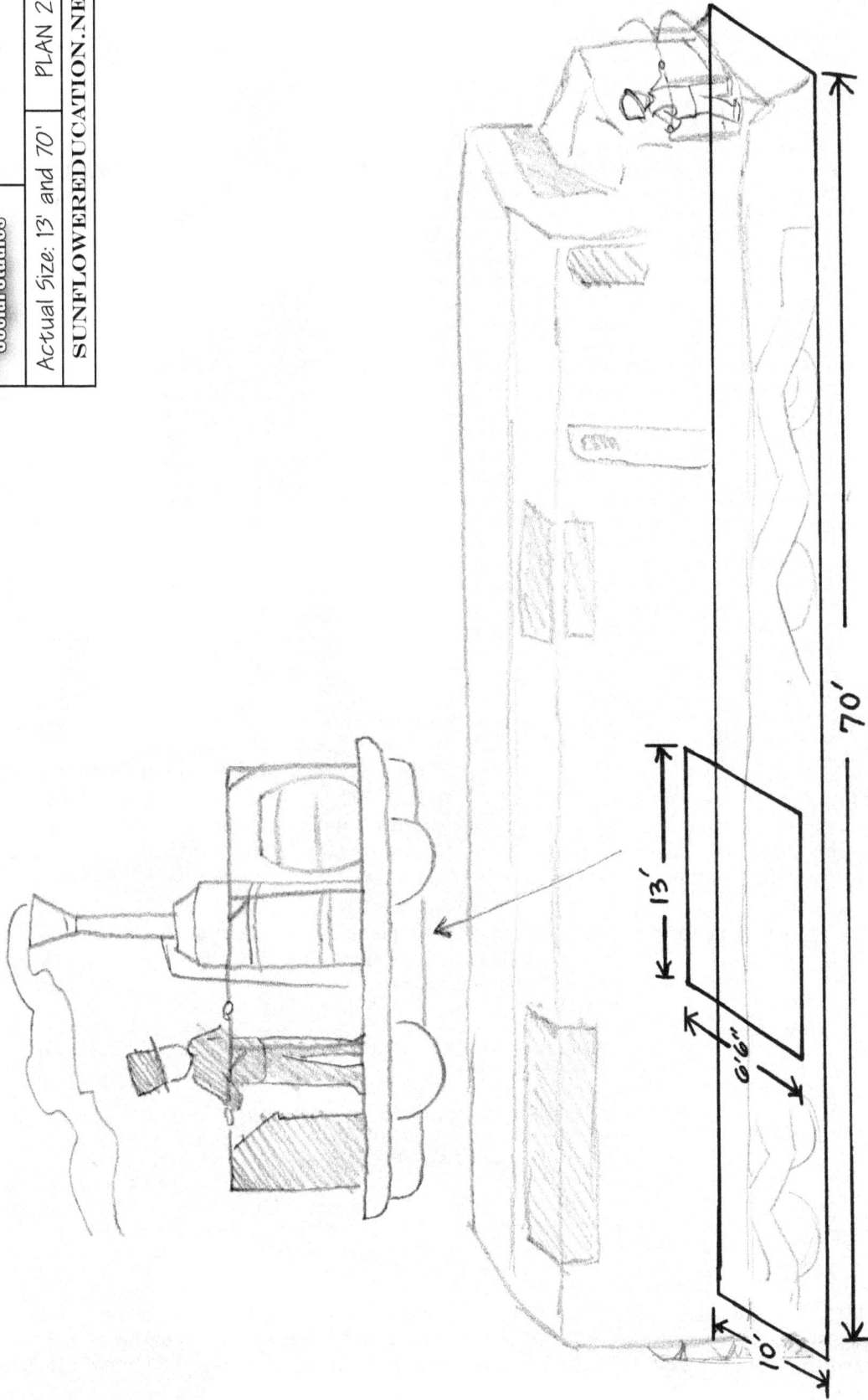

70'

13'

6'6"

10'

The Wright Flyer

Students create the lengths of the Wright Brothers' first flights in order to see how far flight has come.

Prepare

- *Allow time:* approximately 1 hour for this activity
- *Gather materials:* Plan 29, measuring tape or measuring wheel, sidewalk chalk or chalk line, stopwatch

Focus

Discuss with students the ease of transportation by airplane today—how people can fly across the oceans and be in another part of the world in a matter of hours. Then explain to students that in 1903, controlled flight had not yet been accomplished by anyone. Then brothers Orville and Wilber Wright invented the airplane.

Present

❶ Consult Plan 29. On the playground (or appropriate indoor floor), measure out and draw lines that are 120 feet, 200 feet, and 852 feet long using the measuring wheel and chalk line. Have one student stand at the end of each line to emphasize the difference between the three lengths.

❷ Ask students where pilots today sit (in a cockpit, in a chair, with a seat belt, surrounded by windows and metal). Tell students to try to picture what it was like to lay flat between two large connected wings, with a spinning *propeller*, directly behind them, with no glass, no chair, and nothing to protect them from the elements.

❸ Have students run from the beginning of the first line to the end of the first line in 12 seconds (the length of the first flight), then do the same with the third line, but try to run it in 59 seconds. Explain that the two flights that occurred in between the first and last flights were both approximately 200 feet long.

———————————— Vocabulary ————————————

propeller: a mechanical device that propels an airplane by spinning blades through the air

Conclude

Explain to students that in one afternoon, the length of the flight increased from 120 feet to 852, and the time of the flight increased from 12 seconds to 59 seconds. Have students explain or describe how quickly flight progressed in one day and then discuss how much it has advanced in the last 100 years. Point out that the wingspan of a large, modern passenger jet is longer than the Wright Brothers' first flight!

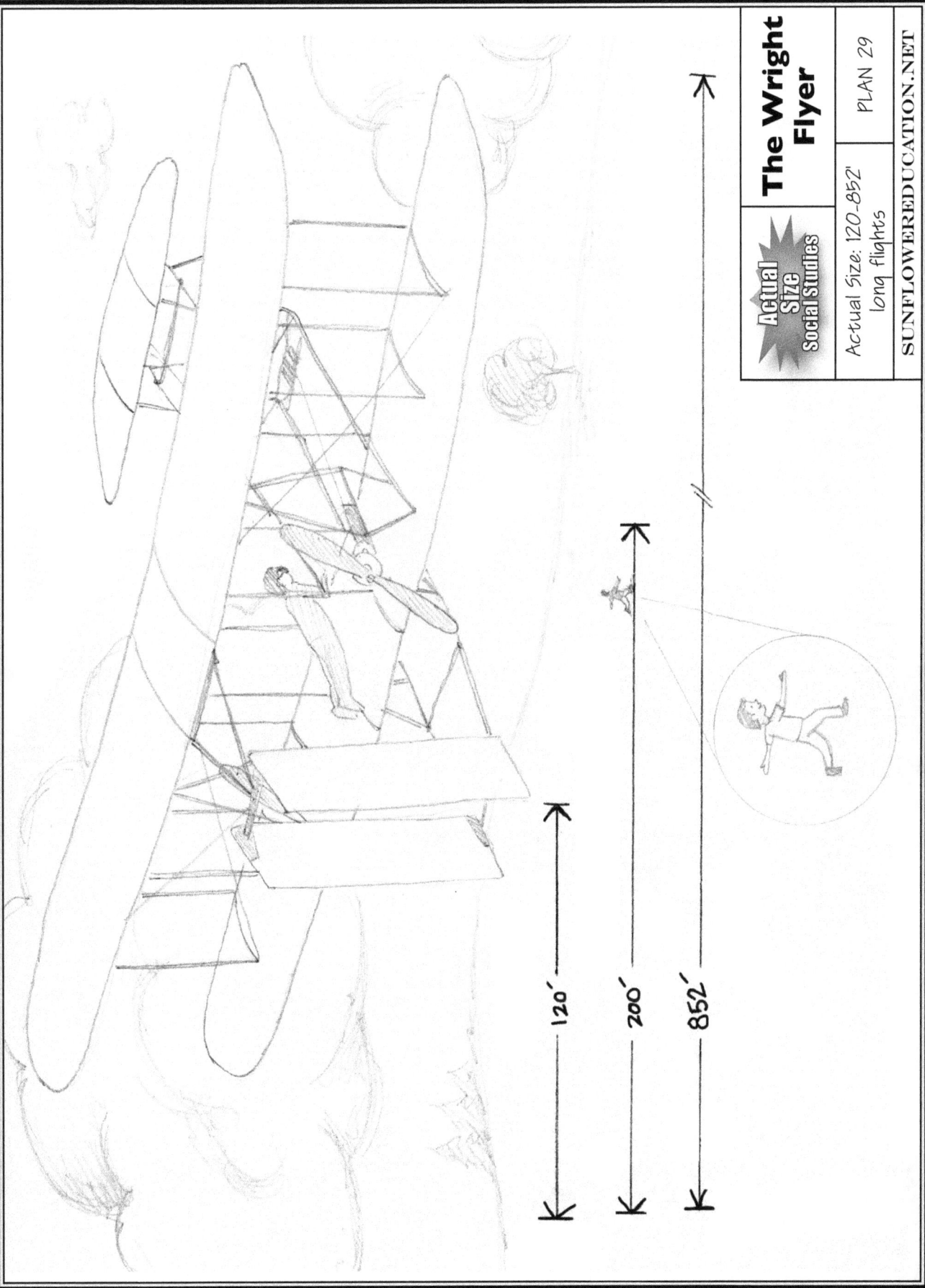

The Wright Flyer

PLAN 29

Actual Size

Social Studies

Actual Size: 120-852'
long flights

SUNFLOWEREDUCATION.NET

852´

200´

120´

Warfare

Range of Weapons

Students draw lines that represent the range of historical and modern weapons in order to better understand military history.

Prepare

- *Allow time:* approximately 1 hour for this activity
- *Gather materials:* Plan 30, measuring tape or measuring wheel, sidewalk chalk or chalk line

Focus

Throughout history, many different kinds of weapons have been used. Over the ages, *technology,* or the way we use science to make tools and machines, has advanced significantly. Since weapons are tools, they have advanced a lot, as well. Discuss with students what this means for people. With better weapons, people have been better able to protect themselves, but warfare has also become more dangerous.

Present

❶ Consult Plan 30. On the playground (or appropriate indoor floor), draw 7 lines *parallel* to each other using the measuring wheel and chalk line, leaving room to stand between each line. The lines should be, from top to bottom, 20, 40, 75, 100, 150, 200, and 225 yards long. These lines represent, from top to bottom, the ranges of a spear, an *atlatl*-thrown dart, a Revolutionary War musket, a Civil War musket, a bow and arrow, a medieval crossbow, and a longbow. Label each line.

❷ Atlatls were used by humans as long as 30,000 years ago to throw darts, or small, sharp pointed objects at a faster speed and for greater distances. A musket is a gun that was not very accurate and which was later replaced by the more accurate rifle. A bow is a curved piece of wood holding a string that used to shoot arrows, or long, thin sticks with a sharp point. A crossbow was used in Medieval times. It is similar to a bow and arrow, except the crossbow is made of a bow fastened to a piece of wood. The longbow is also like a bow and arrow, except that it is taller.

─────────────── Vocabulary ───────────────

technology: using science for practical purposes

parallel: lines that are side by side and have the same distance between every part of themselves

atlatl: a tool used to throw darts farther

Conclude

The longbow's range is much longer than that of the Civil War musket, even though the longbow is a much older weapon. Ask students why people might have wanted to use muskets instead of longbows in the Civil War. Explain to students that it is much easier to make bullets than it is to make arrows and that bullets do more harm than arrows.

20 Yards
Spear

40 Yards
Atlatl

75 yards
Revolutionary War Musket

100 yards
Civil War Musket

150 yards
Bow and Arrow

200 Yards
Medieval Crossbow

225 yards
Longbow

(Modern Infantry Rifle = ~600 yards)

20 Yards

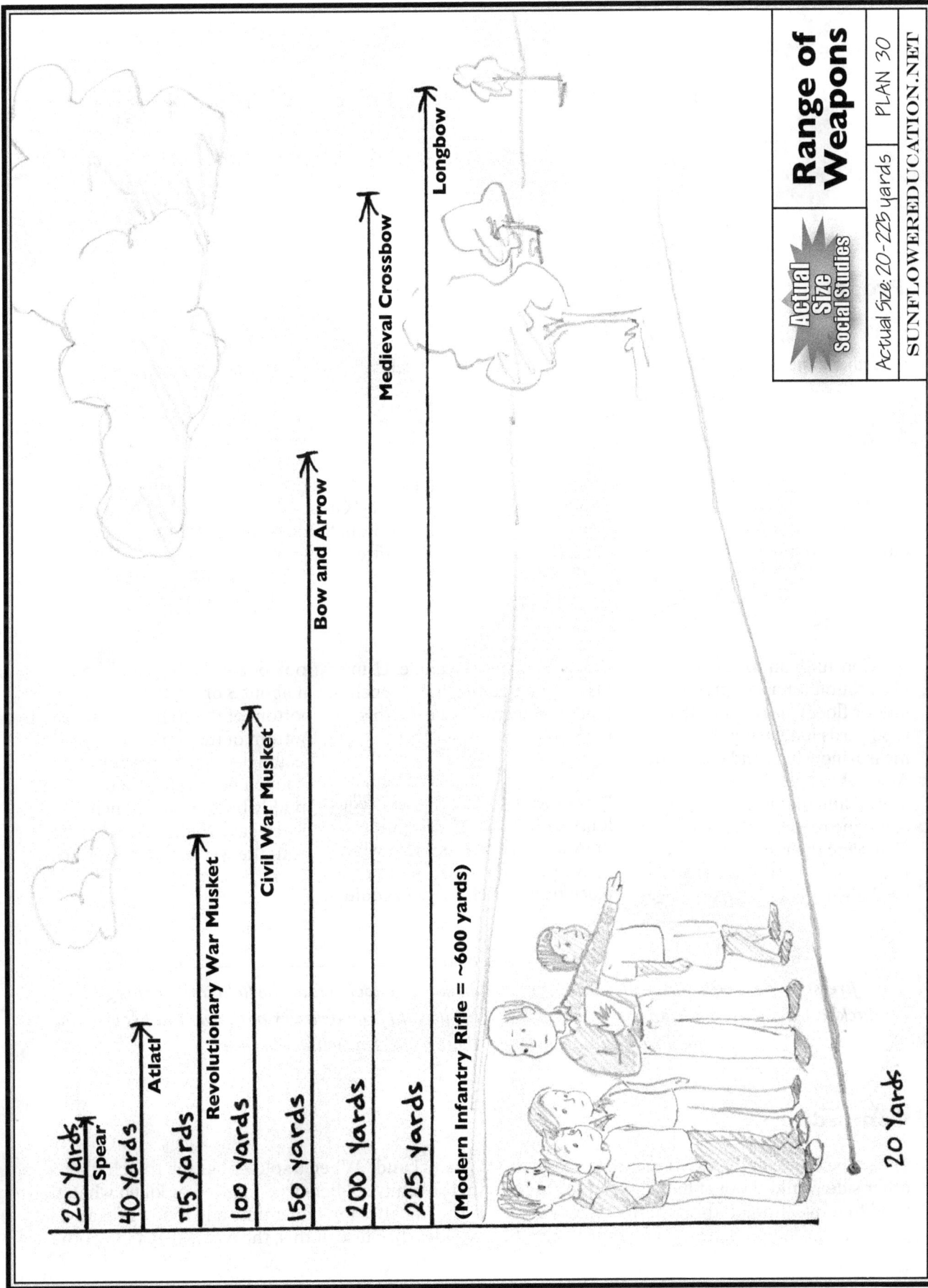

Actual Size
Social Studies

Range of Weapons

Actual Size: 20–225 yards   PLAN 30

SUNFLOWEREDUCATION.NET

World War I Trenches

Students outline a World War I trench in order to learn about trench warfare.

Prepare

- *Allow time:* approximately 1 hour for this activity
- *Gather materials:* Plan 31, measuring tape or measuring wheel, sidewalk chalk, chalk line, carpenter's square

Focus

When World War I began, no one had ever seen anything like it. It was called a "world war" because so many powerful countries were involved. (It was also called the "Great War" at the time.) New and frightening weapons were used, and "trench warfare" was common. Soldiers dug out trenches, or big ditches, so that they would be protected from the enemy's gunfire.

Present

❶ Consult Plan 31. On the playground (or appropriate indoor floor), draw a line that is 30 yards long using the measuring wheel and chalk line. At a right angle to the first line, draw a line that is 30 feet long using the carpenter's square. Complete the rectangle. This represents a small slice of a battlefield. Choose a place near the edge of this rectangle. Using Plan 31 as a guide, draw trenches that are 6 feet wide inside this rectangle.

❷ Next to the first diagram, draw a straight line that is 7 feet long. Using Plan 31 as a guide, draw a trench that is 6 feet wide. Leave room for a *"fire-step,"* a place from which soldiers could look out at the field and fire, at about 3 or 4 feet from the bottom of the trench. Near the bottom of the trench, draw a thin rectangle. This is a *duckboard,* a wooden board placed above the muddy bottom of a trench. This board gave soldiers some relief from the wet and cold ground.

―――――――――― *Vocabulary* ――――――――――

fire-step: a place in a trench where a soldier can stand to look out at the field and fire his gun
duckboard: board made up of several wooden slats used to provide a dry path over muddy ground
stalemate: a situation where there is no clear winner or loser

Conclude

The space between the two trenches was called "No Man's Land." When a soldier left the trench, the other side would shoot at him. Explain to students that so many soldiers were injured or killed when they tried to move through this area that people stayed in the trenches for a long time and didn't gain any ground. This led to many *stalemates* between the two sides. Because of this, the war lasted a long time.

World War I Trenches

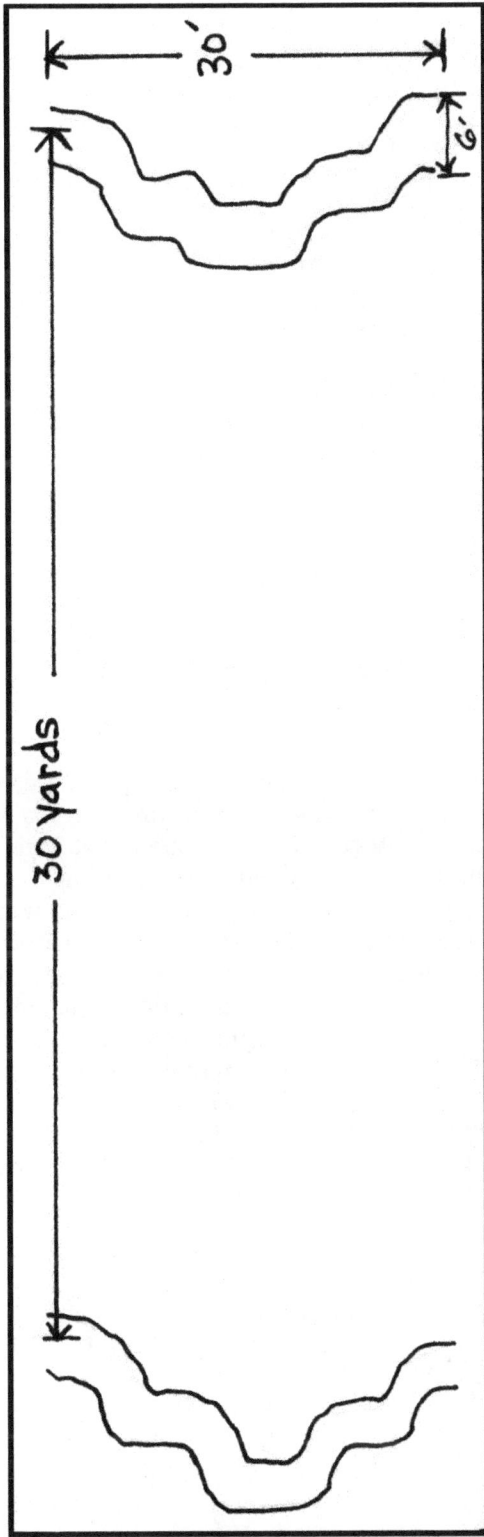

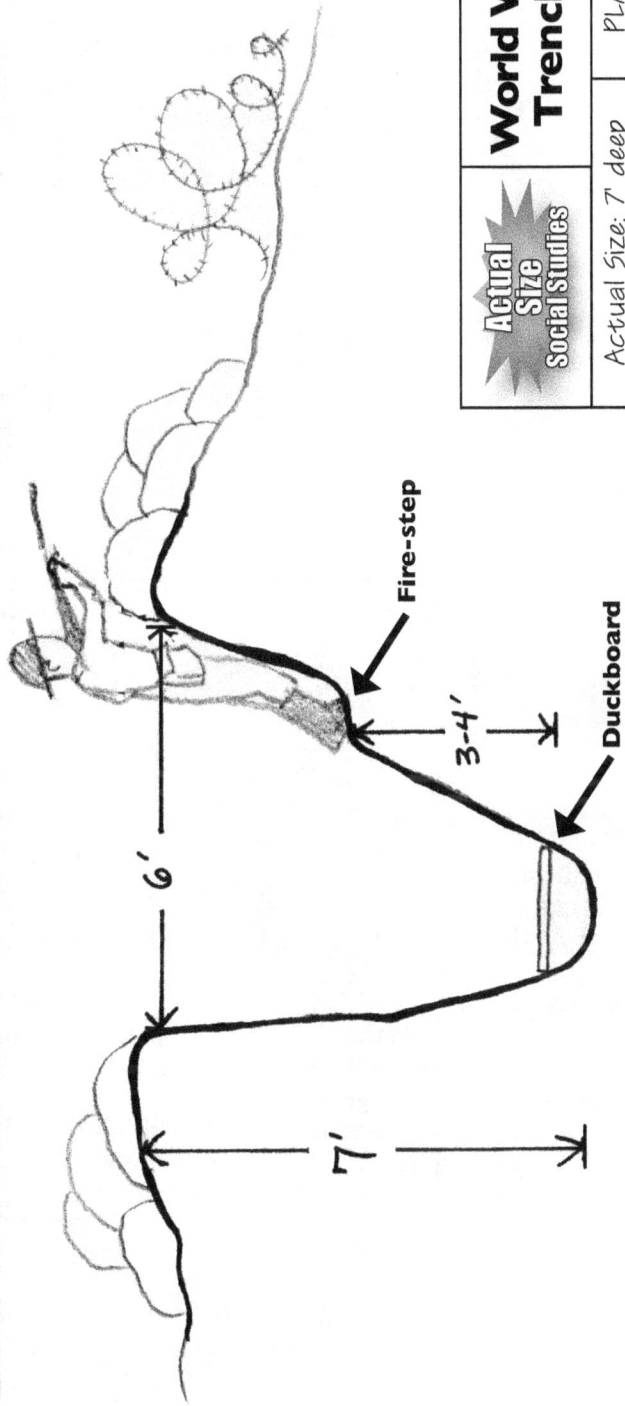

Actual Size: 7' deep

PLAN 31

SUNFLOWEREDUCATION.NET

30 yards

30'

6'

Fire-step

3-4'

6'

7'

Duckboard

Activity 32
Modern Tanks

Students will outline a modern tank in order to help understand today's military.

Prepare

- *Allow time:* approximately 45 minutes for this activity
- *Gather materials:* Plan 32, measuring tape or measuring wheel, sidewalk chalk, chalk line, carpenter's square

Focus

What do a medieval knight and a modern tank have in common? They both wear armor to protect themselves. Tanks, which are *armored* vehicles, were invented during World War I, but they were not used heavily until World War II. Tanks became a very important part of this war.

Present

❶ Consult Plan 32. On the playground (or appropriate indoor floor), draw a 26-foot line using the measuring wheel and chalk line. Draw another, 12-foot line at a right angle to the first line using the carpenter's square. Complete the rectangle. This represents the body of the tank. On the middle of one of the 12-foot lines, draw a rectangle that is 6-feet long and 1-foot wide. This is the tank's gun.

❷ Discuss with students why an army would want to use tanks. Explain that tanks protect the soldiers who are in them from getting hurt, so tanks can move through places that are too dangerous for people on foot. Tanks are also equipped with very powerful weapons that can help an army to win a battle.

❸ Ask students where they would expect to find a tank, on land or on water. Most will

answer, "on land." There were some tanks used during World War II, though, that were *amphibious,* meaning they could go on land or in water. Have students brainstorm about ways a heavy tank could be made to float. Encourage thoughtful answers. Explain to them that these tanks had "flotation screens," which were made of *canvas* and which could be folded up when they weren't needed.

─────── *Vocabulary* ───────

armored: *covered with metal plates for protection*
amphibious: *suited for both land and water*
canvas: *a type of strong cloth*

Conclude

What do students think it would be like to ride inside of a tank? What would it be like to see one while you're on foot? Encourage thoughtful answers.

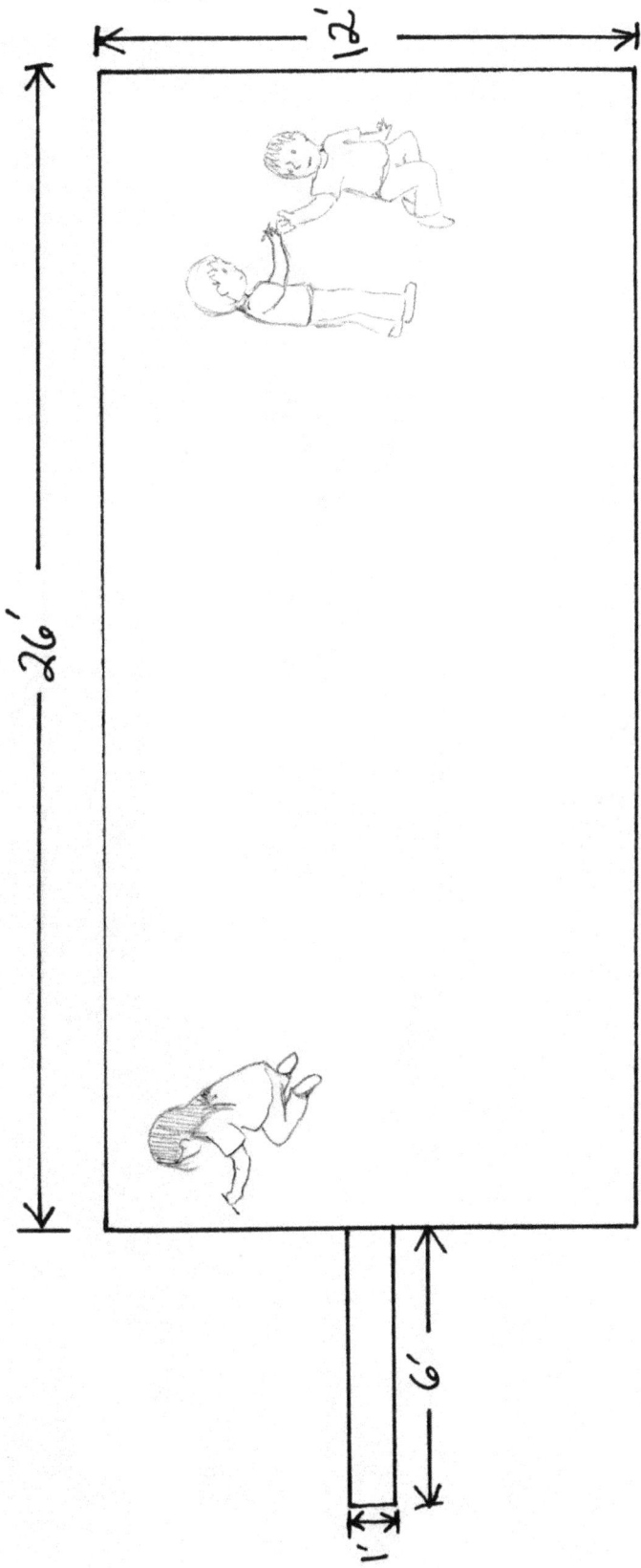

12'

26'

6'

1'

Modern Tanks

PLAN 32

SUNFLOWEREDUCATION.NET

Actual Size
Social Studies

Actual Size: 26' x 12'

American Landmarks

The Alamo

Students create a full-scale map of the Alamo in order to visualize this major landmark of Texas history.

Prepare

- *Allow time:* approximately 1 day for this activity
- *Gather materials:* Plan 33, measuring tape or measuring wheel, sidewalk chalk, chalk line, field chalk liner, carpenter's square

Focus

"Remember the Alamo!" is one of the most famous sayings in American history. During the Texas Revolution, Texan soldiers attempted to defend the Alamo, an old Spanish *mission,* from the Mexican Army. The Texans were trying to declare their *independence* from Mexico. Eventually they succeeded, but it took the sacrifice of many brave soldiers.

Present

❶ Consult Plan 33. Recreating the Alamo is a major undertaking, but doable. You may want to create the outline in half or quarter scale. Follow Plan 33 carefully. Consider placing stakes at the major corners and connecting those with lines made with a professional "field chalk liner" or "field liner," used to mark athletic fields, and possessed by many schools.

❷ Consider organizing students into teams, with captains, who are responsible for various parts of the drawing. Name the teams after Alamo defenders (E.g., the Bowie Team, the Crocket Team). As you work with students, share with them what you know about the Alamo, the battle, the individuals involved, and the aftermath. Quiz and question them informally as you work.

❸ Direct students to make staked signs to identify the various parts of this unique diagram. Prepare students as tour guides and invite local residents and the local media to "Remember the Alamo!" by visiting the site.

———————————— Vocabulary ————————————

mission: headquarters for people who are trying to spread the Christian religion
independence: being free from outside control
commemorate: to show respect for someone's memory

Conclude

There were about 200 Texan soldiers in the Battle of the Alamo, and most of them died. At a later battle in the Texas Revolution, soldiers cried, "Remember the Alamo!" Ask students why they might have said this. Encourage thoughtful answers. Explain to students that they wanted to *commemorate* the soldiers who died at the Alamo and to fight in their names.

The Alamo

PLAN 33

Actual Size: 556'x430'

SUNFLOWEREDUCATION.NET

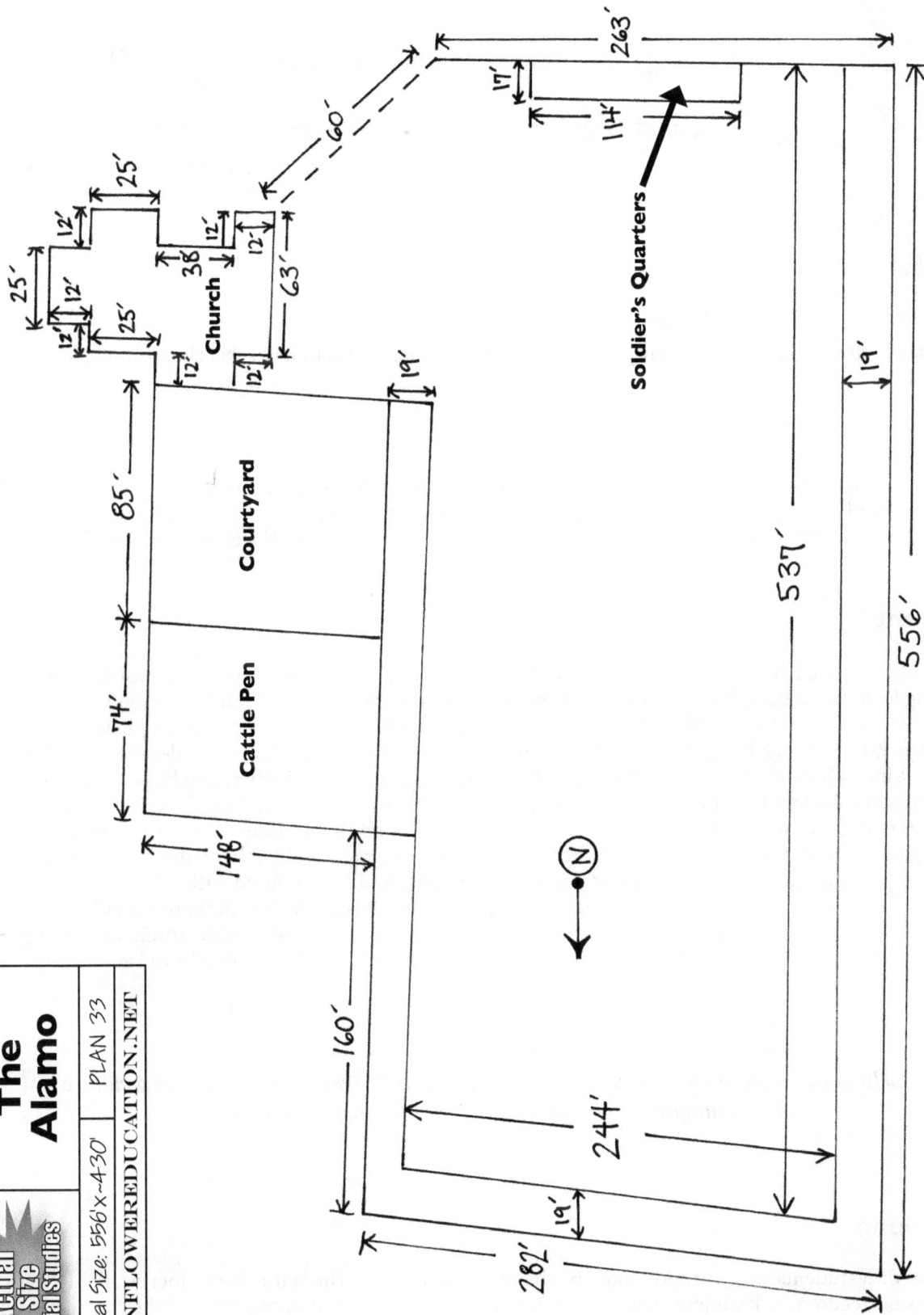

Church

Courtyard

Cattle Pen

Soldier's Quarters

N

263'

60'

25'

12'

25'

12'

25'

12'

25'

38'

12'

12'

63'

12'

12'

17'

114'

19'

85'

74'

148'

160'

537'

556'

244'

19'

19'

282'

The Statue of Liberty's Torch

Students outline the Statue of Liberty's torch in order to grasp the famous monument's impressive size.

Prepare

- *Allow time:* approximately 1½ hours for this activity
- *Gather materials:* Plan 34, measuring tape or measuring wheel, sidewalk chalk, chalk line, carpenter's square

Focus

America is called a *melting pot.* Explain to your students that many different kinds of people live in our country. All of these people's ancestors came from other countries as *immigrants* looking for a better life. Many of them came to New York harbor first, where they were greeted by the Statue of Liberty.

Present

❶ Consult Plan 34. This drawing looks complicated at first, but it can be drawn quickly. Draw the 9-foot, 2-inch by 2-foot, 9-inch rectangle first. Next draw the 12-foot by 4-foot, 6-inch rectangle. Using these two rectangles as a foundation, follow Plan 34 to complete the torch.

❷ This drawing can really benefit from the use of colored chalk. Use yellows and golds for the flame and light green colored chalks for the torch and hand. Further, you might challenge students to sketch Lady Liberty's hand. (For reference: her index finger is about 8 feet long, and her fingernail is 13 by 10 inches.)

❸ As students work, share these fun facts about the Statue of Liberty: overall height (including pedestal) is 305 feet, 6 inches; height of Statue itself is 111 feet, 6 inches; height of face: a little over 8 feet ; in 1986, the flame of the torch was covered with thin sheets of gold. Although there is a ladder up the arm into the torch, visitors are no longer allowed access.

———————————— *Vocabulary* ————————————

melting pot: a place where many different kinds of people live together and share a culture
immigrant: a person who moves from another country

Conclude

Discuss with students what is represented by the Statue of Liberty. The statue is of Libertas, the Roman goddess of freedom. Ask students what the Statue might have meant to immigrants as they came to America. Encourage thoughtful responses.

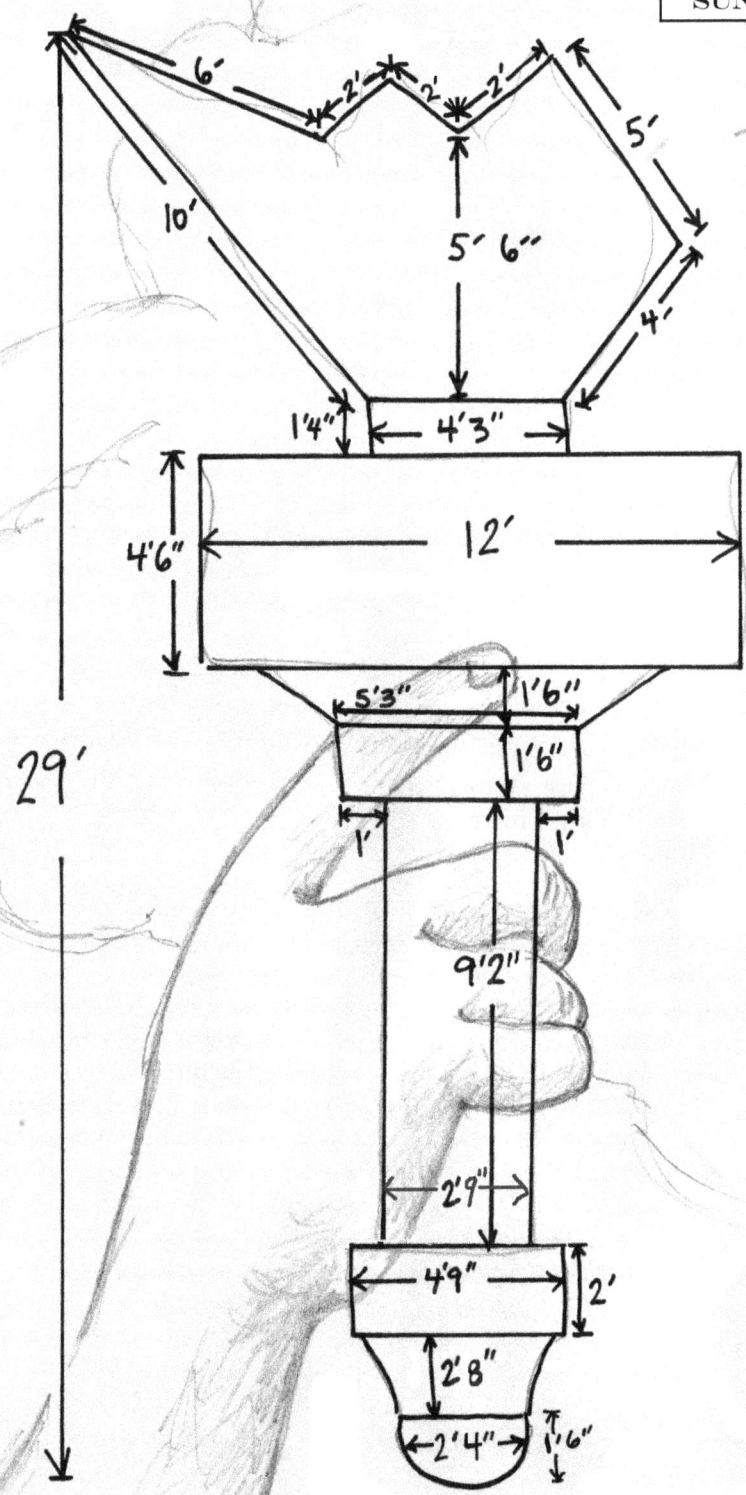

6'
2'
2'
2'
5'
10'
5' 6"
4'
1'4"   4'3"
29'
4'6"   12'
5'3"   1'6"
1'6"
1'   1'
9'2"
2'9"
4'9"   2'
2'8"
2'4"   1'6"

Activity 35
The Oval Office

Students outline the Oval Office in order to visualize this very important room.

Prepare

- *Allow time:* approximately 1 hour for this activity
- *Gather materials:* Plan 35, measuring tape or measuring wheel, sidewalk chalk, chalk line, carpenter's square, stakes (2), string

Focus

What is the most important room in America? The Oval Office! This room, located in the White House, is where the president of the United States works. One can only imagine that many important things happen here. The president is in charge of the *executive branch*, which is the part of the American government that makes sure laws are carried out. The president is also the commander-in-chief of the armed services and the symbolic head of the country.

Present

❶ Consult Plan 35. Notice that the drawing is of an ellipse. To draw the ellipse, use the "gardener's oval" technique, in which a loop of string around two stakes is held taught as it is walked around the stakes, tracing an ellipse. Begin by drawing a line 35 feet, 10 inches long. Measure 7 feet, 5 inches in from each end of the line. These are the locations for the stakes for the ellipse. Use a loop of string 57-feet long to create the correct size and shape.

❷ Show students pictures of different presidents in the Oval Office and, if possible, show students a few clips from speeches made by presidents from the Oval Office. This is also where the president meets with leaders of foreign countries. Ask students why a president would want to do these kinds of things in the Oval Office. Explain to them that this office represents the *authority* and *dignity* of the president, and of the country.

❸ If time permits, let each student sit behind the "desk." Ask them to describe one law they would like to advocate if they were president. Encourage thoughtful responses.

———————————————— Vocabulary ————————————————

executive branch: *the branch of the government that carries out laws*
authority: *the power to lead people*
dignity: *a quality that makes a person worthy of respect*

Conclude

When a new president is elected, he or she gets to redecorate the Oval Office. Ask students to draw pictures of how they would decorate the Oval Office if they were president. Encourage student creativity.

© 2013 Sunflower Education

Actual Size Social Studies

The Oval Office

Actual Size: ~36' x 29' | PLAN 35

SUNFLOWEREDUCATION.NET

Gardener's Oval

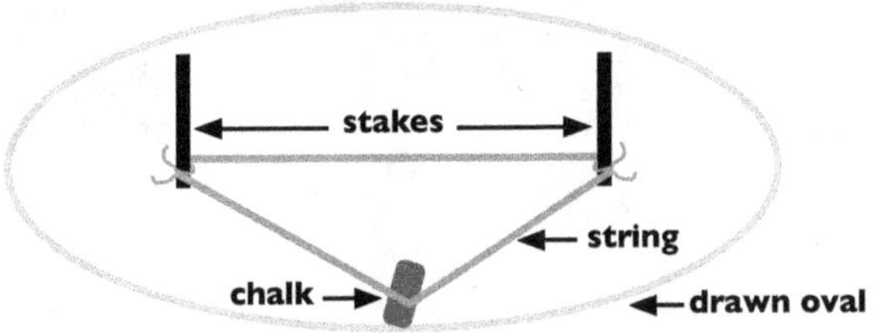

stakes

string

chalk

drawn oval

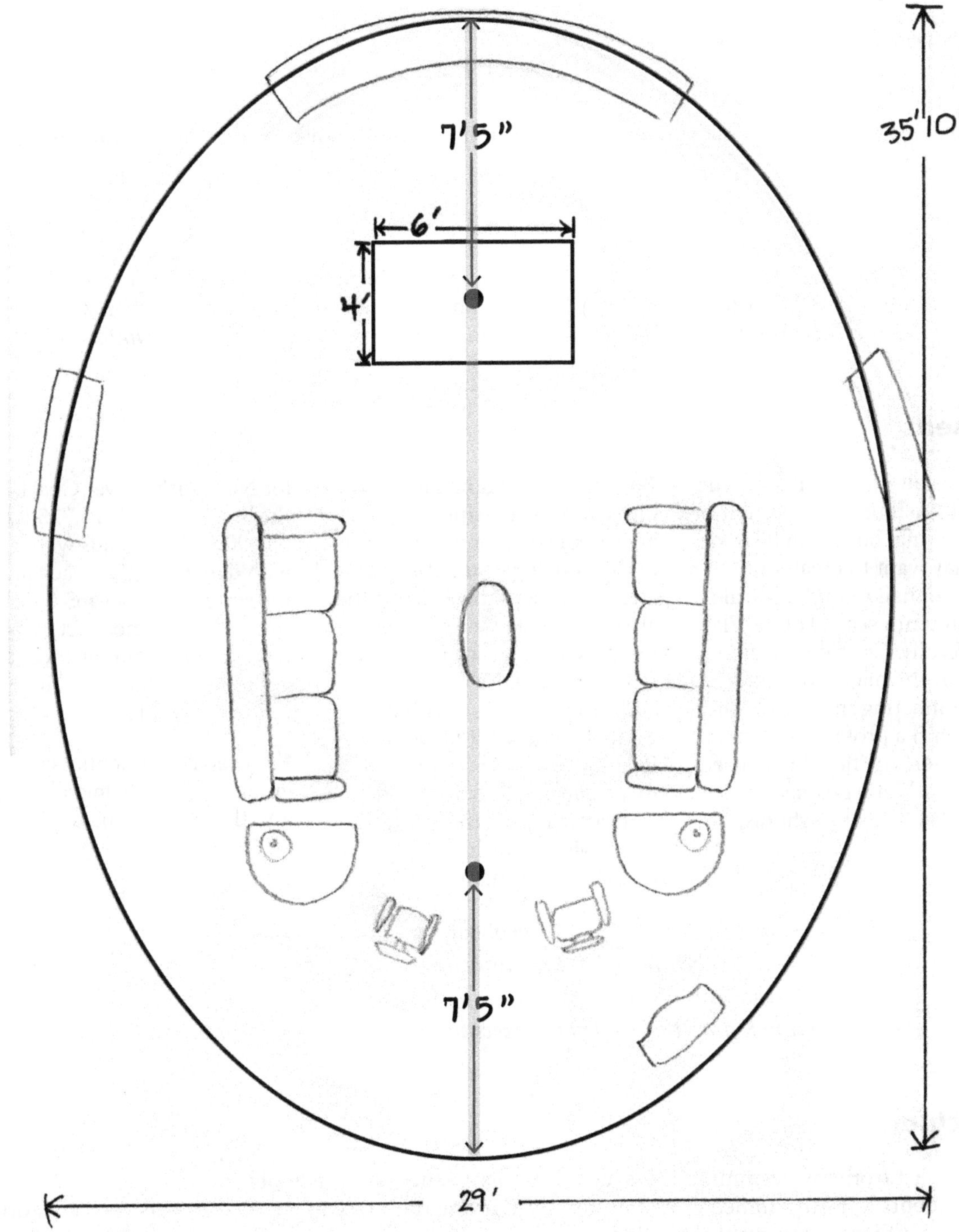

7'5"

6'

4'

35'10"

7'5"

29'

Activity 36
Mount Rushmore

Students outline Mount Rushmore in order to visualize this famous landmark.

Prepare

- *Allow time:* approximately 1 day for this activity
- *Gather materials:* Plan 36, measuring tape or measuring wheel, sidewalk chalk, chalk line, carpenter's square

Focus

Discuss with students who some of the most important people in America's history are. Have students come up with a list of important Americans. Likely on this list will be some presidents. In 1927, construction began on Mount Rushmore in South Dakota to commemorate four *presidents of the United States.*

Present

❶ Consult Plan 36. Recreating Mount Rushmore is an ambitious undertaking, but it can be done. You may want to create the outline in half or quarter scale or even tenth scale. Follow Plan 36 carefully. Consider placing stakes at the major locations and connecting those with lines made with a professional "field chalk liner" or "field liner," used to mark athletic fields, and possessed by many schools.

❷ Consider organizing students into teams, with captains, who are responsible for various parts of the drawing. Name the teams after the part of the drawing they are responsible for defenders (Team Washington, Team Jefferson, etc.). As you work with students, share with them what you know about Mount Rushmore. Quiz and question them informally as you work. Consider sharing these fun facts about Mount Rushmore: Mount Rushmore was named in 1885 for New York lawyer Charles E. Rushmore, and it is 5,725 feet tall; 90% of the heads were carved with dynamite; the heads are to the scale of people 465 feet (47 stories!) tall; almost 400 workers helped the memorial; it cost almost $1 million to build; it was built between 1927 and 1941.

❸ Prepare students as tour guides and invite local residents and the local media to visit your work.

─────────── Vocabulary ───────────

sculpture: *a three-dimensional work of art*
dynamite: *an explosive often used in mining and demolition*
President of the United States: *the head of the executive branch of the government of the United States*

Conclude

Take the list from the beginning of this lesson and have students vote to pick out one person. Brainstorm with students how to commemorate this person. Carving their face into a mountain is probably too big of an idea, but there are many other options that can be displayed in your school or community.

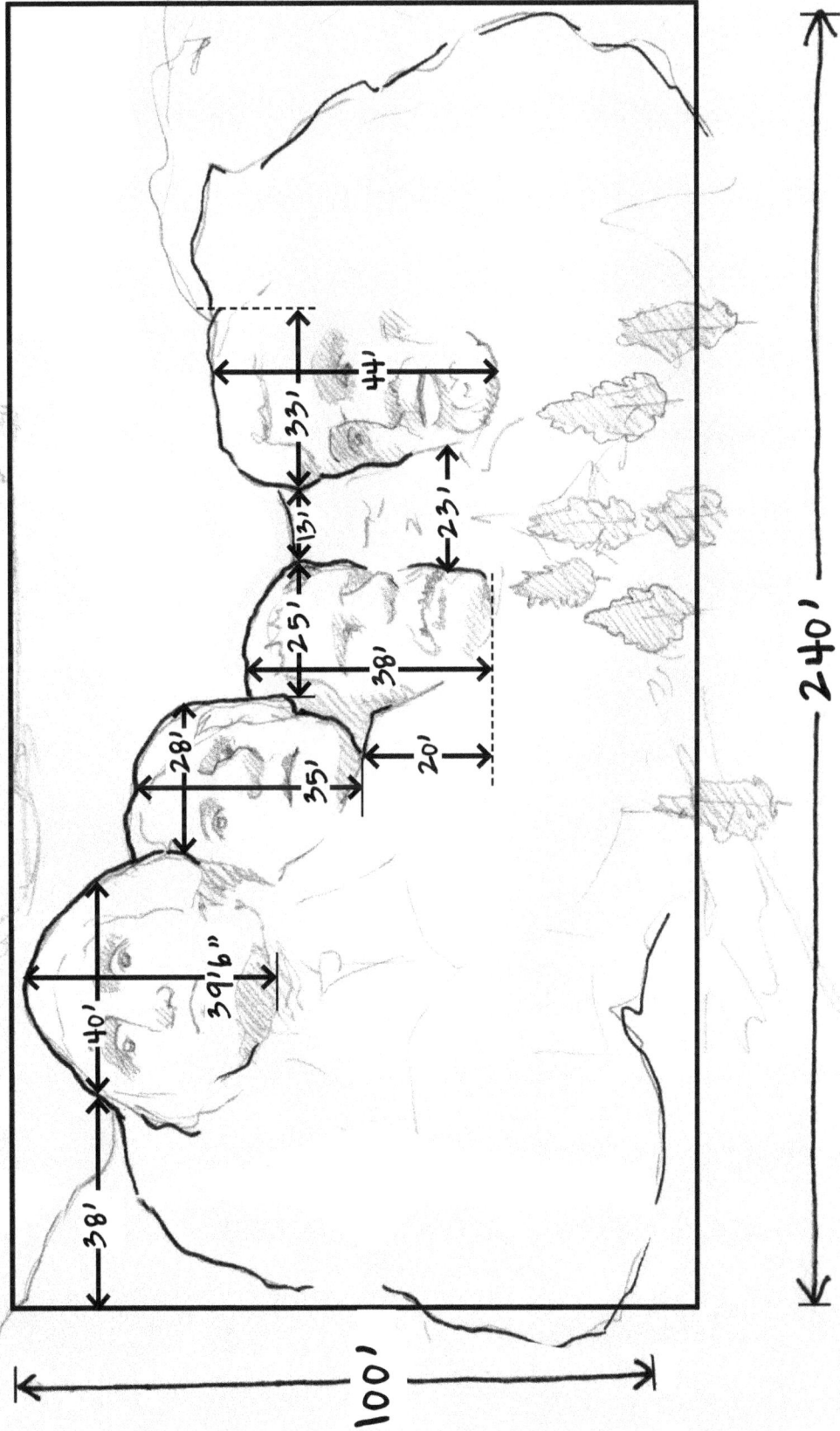

PLAN 36

Actual Size: 60' tall faces

SUNFLOWEREDUCATION.NET

Actual Size
Social Studies

33'

44'

13'

23'

25'

38'

28'

20'

35'

40'

39'6"

38'

240'

100'

www.ingramcontent.com/pod-product-compliance
Lightning Source LLC
Chambersburg PA
CBHW081236090426
42738CB00016B/3328